# MIRADOR

# Mirador
*Vistas from Calvary*

STEVE DIXON

RESOURCE *Publications* • Eugene, Oregon

MIRADOR
Vistas from Calvary

Copyright © 2025 Steve Dixon. All rights reserved. Except for brief quotations in critical publications or reviews, no part of this book may be reproduced in any manner without prior written permission from the publisher. Write: Permissions, Wipf and Stock Publishers, 199 W. 8th Ave., Suite 3, Eugene, OR 97401.

Resource Publications
An Imprint of Wipf and Stock Publishers
199 W. 8th Ave., Suite 3
Eugene, OR 97401

www.wipfandstock.com

PAPERBACK ISBN: 979-8-3852-4018-0
HARDCOVER ISBN: 979-8-3852-4019-7
EBOOK ISBN: 979-8-3852-4020-3

VERSION NUMBER 07/01/25

Unless otherwise stated, the Scripture quotations contained herein are from the New Revised Standard Version of the Bible, Anglicized Edition, copyright © 1989, 1995 by the division of Christian Education of the National Council of the Churches of Christ in the United States of America, and are used with permission. All rights reserved.

Scripture quotations taken from the HOLY BIBLE, NEW INTERNATIONAL VERSION are copyright © 1973, 1978, 1984 by International Bible Society. Used by permission of Hodder & Stoughton, a member of the Hodder Headline Group. All rights reserved.

For Sean Robertshaw—
pastor, colleague, poet and friend.

# Contents

*Introduction* | ix

| | | |
|---|---|---|
| Week 1 | Just Deserts | 2 |
| Week 2 | Unforgivable | 16 |
| Week 3 | In This Together | 30 |
| Week 4 | Positive Regard | 44 |
| Week 5 | Valued Vulnerability | 58 |
| Week 6 | Cosmic Transformation | 72 |
| Week 7 | Vistas from Calvary | 86 |

*Bibliography* | 89

# Introduction

Some years ago, I worked with a young woman who was studying for a master's in theology. The topic of the crucifixion came up in conversation, and it became clear that she understood it solely in terms of "penal substitution"—Jesus takes away the sins of the world by suffering punishment for them in humanity's place. I commented that there were other ways of interpreting the significance of the cross. She seemed perplexed, asking, "What other way is there?" I was surprised, since she was highly intelligent and was studying theology at an advanced level. I gave her a few suggestions off the top of my head and later wondered how many different interpretations there might be. I jotted down as many as I could think of and over time added to my list whenever a new perspective occurred to me, or I came across one in my reading. Eventually, my rough jottings became a collection. To date, I have accumulated thirty-six perspectives. They are presented in this book not as an exhaustive catalogue but as an indication of the rich variety of possible approaches to interpreting the cross and an encouragement to ponder and explore further. As my list grew, I became more formal, recording the sources of new interpretations and I have acknowledged these accordingly. However, my early procedure was lax, and I did not always note whether a thought was my own or someone else's nor, if the latter, what was its source. Even thoughts which I felt were mine have almost certainly occurred to others, so I apologize for any unattributed correspondences and would be grateful to have them pointed out.

## INTRODUCTION

There has never been one agreed Christian understanding of the cross.[1] Of the many possibilities, each age has had its own preferred interpretation, determined by the ethos of the times.[2] It has been suggested that different historical periods have a predominant psychology, shaping their interpretation;[3] and within any given time, the psychology of individuals may have a determining effect on the perspective they take. If Jesus really did die "once *for all*"[4] then the needs of all must be met by the crucifixion, indicating that a sufficient variety of interpretations is required to meet the diversity of human needs. However, many in the church today seem, like my former colleague, to be unaware of any beyond penal substitution. This, together with my growing collection of perspectives, made me think that a book indicating the diversity of other possibilities would be helpful. Not least since the sort of transaction in which Son is a sacrifice offered to Father implies a distance between the two which disrupts the unity of the Trinity.[5]

When I came to analyze my collection into categories, I found that the thirty-six interpretations could be grouped into six themed sets of six, which would provide a six-week study resource, with an interpretation for each day of each week except Sunday. Accordingly, I have set the material out in this format and perhaps, in view of the subject matter, it could be used as a Lent resource, either for individual reflection or in a group setting. However, as the cross is so important for the Christian faith, it could be used at any time and in a variety of contexts.

The themes for my six weeks are:

---

1. See Miller-McLemore, "Practising What We Preach," 56; and van Gend, *Restoring the Story*, which explores four different "stories" of atonement.

2. See Saxbee, *Liberal Evangelism*, 49–50.

3. See Watts, "Lenses on Good Friday" (drawing on Pruyer, "Anxiety, Shame and Guilt").

4. See Eucharistic Prayer A, Archbishops' Council, *Common Worship*, 186. My italics.

5. See Robinson, *The Givenness of Things*, chapter 16.

INTRODUCTION

## Just Deserts

Humanity wants to see wrongdoers punished and this can lead to the "othering" of individuals or groups as offenders who "deserve" to suffer.

## Unforgivable

We do not believe God can forgive us unconditionally and question forgiving others in this way.

## In This Together

Innocent suffering can make us want to punish God. Perhaps God in Jesus accepts this judgement and in sharing human pain holds out a hand to us in solidarity.

## Positive Regard

Rather than being intended to have an effect on God, the purpose of the cross may be to affect us, encouraging self-worth and compassion for others.

## Valued Vulnerability

The self-sacrifice of the cross suggests that unlike human power, divine power lies in vulnerability, offering a view of value that can redeem both individuals and societies.

## Cosmic Transformation

The cross can be seen as the location for a cosmic battle between the powers of light and darkness which transcends human understanding, the outcome of which transforms our view of existence.

## INTRODUCTION

If sin is that which separates us from God and our neighbor,[6] then to say "Jesus died for our sins"[7] can be understood as indicating that he died to heal those separations. The following interpretations of the crucifixion explore how that might be effected. The "sins" for which Jesus died can be seen as largely attitudes of mind that produce a sense of separation from God and our neighbors and even cause fragmentations within ourselves. His death and the reflections to which it can lead perhaps offer routes towards mending these fractures. Each week's material begins with an overview of issues to be raised in the following six days; and each day begins with a prose passage outlining a suggested way of looking at the cross, followed by a pair of brief poems as prompts for further reflection. The first poem outlines a contemporary situation and the second draws on biblical narratives associated with the passion.

If you analyze the structure of the poems, you will find the number seven is important. This is a nod towards the conversation between Matthew's Jesus and Peter regarding forgiveness, in which multiples of seven are significant.[8] I had originally intended to write seventy poems of seven lines each[9], but my material overflowed. There are seventy-three poems rather than the seventy-two you might expect from my six-week framework, since it seemed inconsistent to have only six sections in a collection that gives such prominence to sevens. So, I added a short seventh section, "Vistas from Calvary", containing a brief reflection and just a single poem, by way of an envoi. Perhaps this offers the possibility of a seventh "day" of rest in which to pause and reflect on what has gone before. The final poem has seven lines like its predecessors but breaks from their pattern of seven syllables per line. It also has no rhyme and is not part of a pair. Perhaps these differences might symbolize a breaking out from the constraints of a temporarily imposed

---

6. See the words of The Decision, Archbishops' Council, *Common Worship*, 353. It is a definition I shall use throughout the book.

7. 1 Cor 15:3.

8. Matt 18:22.

9. Reflecting the "seventy times seven" translation.

## INTRODUCTION

discipline in order to move forward—moving on but not totally abandoning what has gone before.

It is common practice to provide questions for discussion at the end of each section of a reflective resource such as a Lent book. However, the questions asked tend to steer the responses given and I would rather each reader found their own course. So, I would encourage you, as an individual or part of a group, to allow issues and questions to emerge which are of relevance to you, and to explore them further in your own way. Follow lines of enquiry that spark your interest and fire your imagination. Let the material connect with your experiences of life and faith and lead you into reflections on them that may challenge, affirm or extend. Use my texts as departure points—conversation starters with others or yourself—and once you have cast off, let the breeze take you wherever it blows.[10] This is not intended as an academic book, but I have provided footnotes and a bibliography for those whom the breeze carries into further explorations.

## Steve Dixon

---

10. See John 3:8.

# Mirador

*Reflections and Poems*

# Week 1
# Just Deserts

Humanity wants to see wrongdoers punished and this can lead to the "othering" of individuals or groups as offenders who "deserve" to suffer.

IN THIS FIRST WEEK we will consider how humanity appears hardwired for revenge as its basic concept of justice.[1] This kills loving forgiveness, and as God is the source of love and forgiveness, if it does not extinguish God entirely, it at least puts a bushel over the light of God within us. The conviction that "someone has to pay" for wrongdoing leads to the belief that for humanity to be forgiven by God for its all-too-obvious shortcomings, someone must be punished. So, blood is not the price of our forgiveness by God so much as the price of our not being able to forgive others. Jesus sacrifices himself not to appease God's bloodlust, but in an attempt to wipe out the sin of our own. Another human trait that feeds into this complex is the sense that suffering is the price of any benefit—you can't have good things "handed to you on a plate". If our forgiveness, redemption, or the coming of the Kingdom are without cost, they must be "too good to be true". However, if we believe this, perhaps we are guilty of the sin of considering God too good to be true.

A kind of moral masochism can make us want to punish ourselves or offer ourselves to be punished for our shortcomings, but

1. Holloway, *On Forgiveness*, explores this.

## WEEK 1 | JUST DESERTS

the urge to punish and make someone pay for the ills of our world is usually aimed at "the other". If it weren't for "them" everything would be fine. This exacerbates alienation from our sister and brother human beings: righteous (us) from unrighteous (them); worthy (us) from unworthy (them). If sin is that which separates us from God and neighbor,[2] then perhaps the cross is a way of saving us from the latter as well as the former part of that dual definition. It is perhaps a way of bringing reconciliation between societies—Jews and Romans shared responsibility for Jesus's death and were equally forgiven; and within a society—both bandit/insurrectionist Barabbas and the crucified thief benefitted from the crucifixion of Jesus.

**Monday** We always want someone to pay for wrongdoing.

**Tuesday** Is seeing blood the price of believing we're forgiven?

**Wednesday** Is there really no gain without pain?

**Thursday** Jesus sets everyone free, whatever their misdemeanors.

**Friday** Worldly judgements of failure are not ultimate.

**Saturday** Humanity is united in its culpability and the forgiveness it receives.

---

2. See *Common Worship*, 353.

## Monday

We always want someone to pay for wrongdoing.

WE WANT SOMEONE TO be sacrificed for "sin"—commonly viewed as the willful wrongdoings of humanity. It seems we always want someone to be punished and "pay" for the cruelty in the world, and the suffering we, and humanity in general, endure as a consequence. And since so much malevolence seems to go unpunished by human systems of justice, we want God to do the job for us: to give the wrongdoers their "just deserts". See the psalms for graphic evidence of this.[3] The Greek that is usually translated in English as "It is finished"—the last utterance of Jesus from the cross, according to John's Gospel[4]—is actually a single word which can be used to indicate "the bill is paid". However, this does not necessarily imply some kind of substitutionary deal: humanity owes, but Jesus pays. The loving alternative to revenge for wrongdoing is forgiveness. If we believe God is loving, and that the Jesus of the gospels—who is supposed to show us how God is—repeatedly proclaimed God's forgiveness, then to expect God to punish on our behalf is to do violence to God's nature. Perhaps the "bill" paid by the corpse on the cross is not that resulting from humanity's sin in general, but rather from the specific sin of trying to make God other than God is. If we want God to be a God who shares our need for vengeance, then we are crucifying the embodiment of loving forgiveness. It is not God who wants someone tortured to death to pay for human wrongdoing, it is us: God's ways are not our ways—God's ways are higher.[5] The "butcher's bill"[6] for our vengefulness is one dead God.

---

3. For example: Ps 3:7; 55:20–23; 58:6–11; 94:1–3.
4. John 19:30.
5. See Isa 55:8–9.
6. A traditional military term for the casualty list after an engagement.

# WEEK 1 | JUST DESERTS

## THE CHARGE SHEET

"What he did pulled out my guts."
"She made a stone of my heart."
"They blew my safe world apart."
Reader, supply the details—
choose from the unending list
of crimes for which we insist
someone pays with blood and nails.

## BUTCHER'S BILL

What was torn with whiplash cuts,
spat upon and laughed to scorn,
made to wear the savage thorns,
beaten with unsparing rod
was forgiveness. Escape map
hanging like a bloody scrap—
a butcher's bill: one dead God.

## Tuesday

Is seeing blood the price of believing we're forgiven?

CRUCIFIXION IS HORRIFIC, THOUGH some images of the crucifixion of Jesus fail to show this fully. A loincloth almost always hides the nakedness which was an added degradation for crucifixion victims to endure, but the artists can be equally coy about the awful physical suffering involved. The bloodshed is minimized, the wounded side a mere scratch; the results of the crown of thorns a few red beads; the face of Jesus is shown in sad repose, and the body hanging limp, almost relaxed. However, the writhing hands in Matthias Grünewald's sixteenth-century depiction[7] tell a different story. Even there, though, the image is static, and we don't hear the screams. Mel Gibson's film *The Passion of the Christ* tried to remedy this by showing the true horror of crucifixion. It was too much for some. The world of the first-century Roman Empire would perhaps have been more hardened to brutality than the audiences for Gibson's 2004 film, but crucifixion would surely have been horrific even then. That was the point. It was supposed to be shocking—a severe deterrent to any rebellion against Roman power. And maybe this crude "aversion therapy" hints at another possible significance of the crucifixion. Perhaps it suggests the cross might be a way of trying to put an end to humanity's seemingly insatiable hunger for a bloody reckoning as the price of forgiveness by shocking us out of it. Maybe it could lead us to imagine Jesus saying, "Okay, if you really want to see someone stripped naked, screaming in agony and smeared in blood before you'll believe you're forgiven, then let it be me. But let that be an end of it. Let me be the last."

---

7. Part of the Isenheim Altarpiece, displayed at the Unterlinden Museum, Alsace.

## WARNING

"Prove you love me!" The wild cry
of the lost who cannot see
how they could possibly be
worthy of lover or friend.
Beware demands born of fear:
love-torn Vincent's severed ear[8]
warns how proving love may end.

## AVERSION

Me—I shouted, "Crucify!"
It's what I thought I wanted.
Perhaps that want was planted
by others, but it was me
who ran to see him atone—
gaped in horror at his groans,
vomited, brought to my knees.

---

8. The artist Vincent van Gogh cut off part of his ear and gave it to a girl who cleaned at the local brothel. It has often been interpreted as a bizarre love token, though the mutilation may have been connected to a quarrel with his friend and fellow artist Paul Gauguin.

## Wednesday

Is there really no gain without pain?

THERE IS A PERSISTENT human view that some kind of suffering must precede any good: no gain without pain, and the greater the good, the greater the suffering that must precede it. The sentiment has been repeated many times down the centuries and perhaps goes back to the formation of the human psyche. The theologian, philosopher, physician, and Lutheran minister Albert Schweitzer had an interpretation of the passion which drew on ancient Jewish apocalyptic beliefs. These held that "tribulations" must precede the coming of God's Kingdom. Schweitzer suggested Jesus perhaps came to think that since the Kingdom had not yet come, he must undergo the required tribulations himself to hasten the event. In accepting suffering, Jesus would thus be "a ransom for many".[9] Whether or not Jesus did in fact hold this apocalyptic belief, Schweitzer's use of it offers the possibility that the cross could deliver us from the conviction that we must undergo trauma for God's Kingdom to come. If Jesus did not believe great suffering must precede a great good, others clearly did and still do. Perhaps we might imagine Jesus saying to them, "I tell you the truth, God does not require pain before gain. But if I can't convince you of that, let the pain be mine. And may you accept that God's Kingdom is yours."

---

9. Mark 10:45. I have drawn details of Schweitzer's interpretation from Cupitt, *The Sea of Faith*, 105.

WEEK 1 | JUST DESERTS

## SUSPICIOUS

This must be some kind of scam:
"Click at once to claim your prize."
I don't gamble. It's not wise,
or honest. Only hard toil
produces food I dare eat.
These baskets piled at my feet
are fruit from some poisoned soil.

## TRIBULATION

If you think a door must slam
on the day, shut up the sun,
or some such tribulation
fall for blessings to be sent,
let the cross have that effect—
let the mayhem you project
be this murdered innocent.

## Thursday

Jesus sets everyone free, whatever their misdemeanors.

WANTING TO SEE SOMEONE punished for sin can lead to an "othering" of the sinner on the part of those who fail to acknowledge that they too share in human frailty. This is reflected in a phenomenon psychologists describe as "fundamental attribution error". This is our instinctive assumption that when *we* get something wrong, it's due to extenuating circumstances but when *someone else* gets something wrong, it's because they're a bad/foolish/"failed" person.[10] One consequence of Jesus's crucifixion was the release of the prisoner Barabbas—variously described as notorious;[11] a rebel, insurrectionist, and murderer;[12] and a bandit.[13] His release could be regarded as a sign against "othering": a symbolic event indicating that Jesus sets everyone free, whatever the nature or tally of their misdemeanors. Interestingly, the name Barabbas means "son of the father"—a reminder perhaps that all are children of the same heavenly parent and siblings of Jesus. Some variant texts even give Barabbas the additional name Jesus—calling him "Jesus Barabbas"—further hinting at identification rather than alienation. To the symbolism of Barabbas's release, we could add the "harrowing of hell"—the traditional account of Jesus's activity between his crucifixion and resurrection. If hell is a symbolic holding pen for those subject to the ultimate "othering", then the harrowing underlines that whatever the death of Jesus offers, it offers to all. The proclamation of "release to the captives"[14] applies to every member of flawed humanity.

---

10. Hayes, *What Are You Thinking?*, 56.
11. Matt 27:16.
12. Mark 15:7; Luke 23:19, 25; Acts 3:14.
13. John 18:40.
14. Luke 4:18. (referencing Isa 61:1 and 58:6).

# WEEK 1 | JUST DESERTS

## UNRECOGNIZABLE

"Beast! Fiend! Monster! Animal!"
Banners and a howling crowd.
A shrunken figure, head bowed,
is hustled into the dock.
His mother, wife and brother
in the gallery smother
recognition, jaws like rock.

## IDENTITY

"Friend, who is that criminal?"
"Jesus, son of the Father,
crucified. Said he'd rather
keep his peace, so made no plea."
"And who's that fellow reeling,
arms wide, as if appealing?"
"Jesus, Father's son, set free."

## Friday

Worldly judgements of failure are not ultimate.

THE "NOTORIOUS" JESUS BARABBAS may have been set free as a result of the crucifixion of Jesus of Nazareth, but there were two others, whose description is variously translated as rebels, revolutionaries, thieves, robbers, brigands, bandits, outlaws, criminals, or simply bad men, who did go to their deaths on Golgotha alongside the Nazarene.[15] They were not spared their earthly fate, and one of them acknowledged that it was a fate they deserved. This is often interpreted as penitence, although it could be no more than simple realism. However, penitent or not, this crucified criminal asked Jesus to remember him when he came into his kingdom and Luke's Jesus assured him that they would be together in paradise.[16] If Jesus's fellow victims were any of the things the translations suggest, they would be regarded by many as having failed in life. And even for someone who rejoiced in their criminal calling, to be captured and put to death in this most degrading way must be seen as a failure, if only a failure to "get away with it". And, of course, to be crucified, especially by the Romans, was a sure sign of a failed messiah. The story of Jesus and his two companions on the hill is, therefore, one of fellow failures in the eyes of the world. And yet, Jesus and the one who asks to be remembered by him are both elevated to paradise—a destination traditionally regarded as the ultimate sign of success. This consequence of Jesus's crucifixion shows that earthly judgements are neither reliable nor final: the lowest may yet be raised to the highest[17] and success snatched from the jaws of failure.

---

15. Matt 27:38; Mark 15:27; Luke 23:33; (also John 19:18, although this does not identify them as criminals). Bible Gateway indicates the variety of translations https://www.biblegateway.com/

16. Only recorded by Luke, champion of the outsider: Luke 23:40–43.

17. See Matt 20:16.

# WEEK 1 | JUST DESERTS

## CONDEMNATION

I was sacked three months ago.
"You're rubbish. Finished," they said.
Those words stay stuck in my head.
My partner hammered them home,
brought up everything I'd done
or not done since we'd begun,
finger like a metronome.

## THE SOLDIER'S OBSERVATION

If there's one thing that I know
it's that no one wins a crown
by getting themselves cut down
in battle, or anything
by bleeding out on a cross;
but this dying human dross
murmurs mercy like a king.

# Saturday

Humanity is united in its culpability and the forgiveness it receives.

IF SIN IS ABOUT separation—from our neighbors, from God and even within ourselves—then the "will to punish" which we have explored this week can be seen as a prime example. We "other" people by condemning them. We "other" God from God's true nature by suggesting a divine need to punish. We create a division in the indivisible divine by creating a story in which God punishes God's self. And we even create a separation in ourselves by feeling we must be punished before we can be loved. We have seen how the cross can be regarded as working against these sins of separation by obliging us to recognize them for what they are.

One obvious and catastrophic "othering" in the world is that between races and we will end the week by considering how the cross may help us see beyond the "blame game" between peoples. Ephesians speaks of the cross bringing together both Jews and Gentiles.[18] Who was to blame for the death of Jesus? By portraying the Jews as calling for the crucifixion of Jesus when given the choice of releasing him or a bandit, the gospel accounts place the responsibility with them. And Matthew underlines the point by describing them as taking it on their own heads and those of their children.[19] But equally, the Gentile Romans bear responsibility. They alone had the power to administer the death penalty;[20] and their representative, Pilate, despite seeing that Jesus was innocent, caved in to pressure and "washed his hands" of the matter. Perhaps since both Gentiles and Jews shared responsibility for the execution of Jesus, both are united as subjects of Jesus's prayer for forgiveness from the cross.[21] By suffering at the hands of his people and also taking in

---

18. Eph 2:11–18.

19. Matt 27:25: a verse that regrettably has been misused to fuel anti-Semitism down the centuries.

20. See John 18:31.

21. Luke 23:34.

WEEK 1 | JUST DESERTS

his own body the suffering inflicted on his people by the Romans, then praying for a general forgiveness, Luke's Jesus was perhaps opening the possibility of healing between the nations through the culpabilities and forgiveness they share.[22] In this connection, it is intriguing to note Luke's comment that tetrarch and governor, previously enemies, became friends after their parts in condemning Jesus to death.[23]

## INTERNECINE STRIFE

Both claimed justice at the start:
rebels and authorities
proclaimed their priorities
were the common good. The waste—
boundless wreck of smashed abodes.
Last one standing stares, reloads,
chokes on triumph's dusty taste.

## ENEMY'S ENEMY

Heaviness in sky and heart
that dark Friday afternoon.
The tetrarch sucks his gold spoon,
the governor his stylus.
Suddenly, a lance of light
slices gloom—a streak of white
illumines both. Forgiveness?

---

22. See Holloway, *On Forgiveness*, and also John's comments on the unconsciously prophetic words of Caiaphas (John 11:52).
23. Luke 23:12.

# Week 2
# Unforgivable

*We do not believe God can forgive us unconditionally and question forgiving others in this way.*

In our first week, we reflected on humanity's reluctance to recognize that God is inherently forgiving. In this second week we go deeper into the implications of this, by examining our responsibility for any rift between humanity and God. Forgiveness is the heart of the Good News—God's forgiveness of us, and the calling to be equally forgiving towards others. Our sin in relation to this is twofold: a manifest failure in the latter, which separates us from neighbor, but also a failure to believe in the former, which separates us from God. It is not God that puts a rift between us, but we ourselves who do this. The death of Jesus can therefore be seen as providing ways to help mend this rift and draw us as close to God as we are meant to be.

Preaching God's unconditional forgiveness was no more popular in the time of Jesus than it is today. It was one of the factors that led the Jewish religious authorities to seek his execution. The fact that his death was not the end of his story perhaps indicates this message of divine forgiveness cannot be put to death, however much the difficulty of forgiving others may make us want to do this. The fact that Luke's Jesus went to his death calling on God to forgive, also challenges us to wish that those who do us harm may be forgiven by God, even though we cannot offer them our own forgiveness. Such a wish can perhaps begin to close the separation between us and those neighbors who have done us harm. However, to go further and actually forgive them ourselves—especially to forgive unconditionally—entails considerable personal cost and the agony suffered by Jesus is a reminder to take seriously the pain involved, especially when we suggest forgiveness to others who have been harmed.[1] Humanity tends to wish those who have caused others pain to suffer as a result. The gospels could perhaps be seen as suggesting that by submitting to a painful death on the cross God in Jesus would rather bear suffering than have it inflicted on any of us.

**Monday** Any rift with God is in our minds, not in the mind of God.

**Tuesday** Preaching love can have dangerous consequences.

**Wednesday** Killing the messenger can't kill the message.

**Thursday** Who has the right to advocate forgiveness?

**Friday** Forgiving has a terrible cost.

**Saturday** "I'd rather it happened to me."

---

1. See Cherry, *Unforgivable?* for a detailed exploration of the complexities of advocating forgiveness.

## Monday

Any rift with God is in our minds, not in the mind of God.

IF THE SIN FOR which Jesus died is our failure to believe that God loves and forgives us whatever we do—the sin of believing that a penalty must be paid for our shortcomings—then Jesus paid the price of an agonizing death not because God ordained it, but because humanity did. We bear responsibility because of our failure to recognize God's true nature. Paul's words to the Christian community at Colossae hint at this analysis of the origin of our separation from God, our true "original sin": "Once you were alienated from God and were enemies *in your minds* because of your evil behavior."[2] Any rifts are in *our* minds, not God's—it is us who feel God must have to punish humanity, not God. And so, it is our minds that must change, be redirected, transformed. Perhaps this is the repentance, the metanoia, to which we are called by the cross.

So many people both outside and within the Christian community have asked the question, "Why did Jesus have to die?" This is particularly the case in modern society where penal substitution, though easy to explain, seems so hard to justify. At one level, there were practical, political reasons for the crucifixion; but there is a further question to ask, which has been equally baffling to many, especially since the Christian faith has given such a vital importance to Christ's death: "What did the crucifixion achieve? From what did it save us?" If the cross was the only way to transform our understanding of God, then perhaps that gives a deeper explanation than either ancient politics or a punishment model of human-divine relations for its "necessary" role in our salvation story. What were we saved from? Perhaps the answer is simply—from ourselves.

---

2. Col 1:21 (New International Version). My italics.

## WEEK 2 | UNFORGIVABLE

### RESPONSIBILITY

"You can't love me anymore."
"I'm not good enough for you."
"I always wreck everything."
Self-defeated, they retreat
from their lovers' longing arms,
blinded by self-pity's pain,
deafened by their own lament.

### RESTRAINING ORDER

Arms to hug and reassure;
hands to nurture and renew;
feet that would hasten to bring
tidings that love gently greets
blemishes as well as charms:
all these by hard spikes restrained,
hammered by our discontent.

## Tuesday

Preaching love can have dangerous consequences.

A WORLD WHICH SEES justice in terms of retribution has often expected God to wield the rod of punishment when human systems have failed to do so. To proclaim that God is not, after all, the ultimate enforcer of punishment, but rather an endless source of unconditional forgiveness and love, is to rob humanity of its last hope of retribution. It is salt in the wounds of the wounded and is received as an insult by the injured.[3] Pain causes a violent response, and the pain caused by the suggestion that there will be no ultimate punishment of wrongdoers has always caused a fierce reaction. So has the "presumption" of those who claim to know the mind of God—but only, it seems, when the "mind" they proclaim differs markedly from that which a society has come to expect. How often are those who declare God to be a God of vengeance denounced as presumptuous in making their claim?

These things were as true of first-century Jewish society as they are of our own today. Jesus was crucified in his day by those who could not tolerate his proclamations of God's unconditional forgiveness and love. Those who repeat them today may not be physically crucified, but they frequently face a hostile response. The bold declarations of forgiveness made by the Jesus of the gospels[4] were denounced as blasphemy[5] and can thus be seen as contributing to his condemnation and execution—a warning of the possible consequences of preaching God's love. His death was the price he was prepared to pay for telling us that any rift with God is not of God's making. It meant that much to him. And it can inspire us with courage to face the consequences of standing up for a belief in divine love, as Jesus did in the gospel accounts.

---

3. Although it does not negate the necessity of continuing to seek human justice when wrong has been done.

4. See Matt 9:2; Mark 2:5; Luke 5:20; also Luke 7:48; and John 8:11.

5. Matt 9:3; Mark 2:6–7; Luke 5:21.

# WEEK 2 | UNFORGIVABLE

## THE PRICE

Those with wealth enough are few:
from whose hearts molten gold sprang
like a fountain, love's elite;
or who on bended knee panned
far-off streams of mercy's flow
to pay the price we exact
from those who preach love divine.

## LONG TIME COMING

"Your sins are forgiven you."
The man rolled up his mat. *Bang.*
The woman's tears bathed his feet.
*Bang.* He bent and wrote in sand.
"I do not condemn you. Go."
*Bang*—the hammer's harsh impact.
*"Forgives? We say God declines!"*

## Wednesday

Killing the messenger can't kill the message.

"Don't shoot the messenger!" is the cry of someone who knows they are bringing news the recipient will not want to hear. It is a recognition of the negative response which information is likely to receive if it doesn't match the hearer's image of how they want their world to be. Psychologists identify unconscious tactics we deploy to avoid or ignore challenging information, giving them self-explanatory titles such as "Confirmation Bias" and "Defense Mechanism".[6] We also use conscious means of blocking out or silencing unwelcome information. We deliberately don't read certain things, don't watch certain programs, don't talk to certain people, only follow "posts" that support our views. Legislation has had to be created in recent times to counter the age-old tactic of threatening to sanction whistle-blowers if they don't keep quiet. As ever, children illustrate this human trait in a naked form which shows such behavior for what it is when they cover their ears and run about chanting nonsense to block something they don't want to hear. Perhaps the truth they tell adults about themselves provides one reason children were traditionally told to be seen and not heard.

If his proclamations of God's forgiveness helped bring Jesus to the cross, could that fate be an extreme example of a society attempting to silence someone who offers a comfort it is not ready to receive—that God is a God of forgiveness not of punishment? The cross is not the end of the story—it is part of a continuum leading to the resurrection and beyond. Could the resurrection that will follow the cross be a way of saying that killing the messenger cannot kill the message? Nothing can kill God's forgiveness because nothing can kill God's love. After all, since God is love,[7] to do so would be to extinguish God's very being.

---

6. See Hayes, *What Are You Thinking?*, 35–36, 37, 207–10.
7. 1 John 4:16.

## REDACTION

A gallows speech cut short by
the rattle of kettle drums;
billows of blinding smoke bloom
from a funeral pyre of print;
a prison van, dark windows,
boxing all words of dissent;
blank TV screens, martial band.

## NOISE

Ever since that, "Crucify!"
chanted by the crowd, what comes
to mind is deafening noise—boom
of bellowed orders; harsh dint
of hammer; screams with each blow.
His end was almost silent—
whispered words, water on sand.

## Thursday

Who has the right to advocate forgiveness?

It is one thing to uphold the principle that all sins can be forgiven and to support it in abstract debate or when calling for mercy in specific instances that don't concern us directly. But what happens when the issue becomes personal? When the wrong in question is a wrong done to us or our nearest and dearest? So often today, when great harm has been done to individuals and families—by violence or deceit—those affected will take to social media to express their grief and outrage, or the news media will give them space to do so. If a perpetrator is brought to justice, the family's "impact statement" is now, rightly, a routine part of proceedings and has its place in influencing the ultimate judgement. It is hard enough for someone outside that family circle, their friends and supporters, to hear such testimony and to suggest that the perpetrator of the wrong might be forgiven. But if one is, oneself, the sufferer of such personal or familial pain it can seem impossible or even improper to consider forgiveness. This is when the challenge is at its most acute—when principle meets practice and is tested to the utmost. It is often said that those who stand on the sidelines and advocate forgiveness have no right to do so: only those suffering the pain of an injury can have that right—or perhaps, those who have suffered a similar agony themselves.

Perhaps that is why the crucifixion has been described as the act in which Jesus made a "perfect" sacrifice for sin.[8] The sin in question is separation not just from our wrong-doing neighbors in general, but from those of them in particular who have done us personal harm. It is also separation from God, in that it rejects the possibility God may already have forgiven them. If they have been "released" in this way, we want a retrial, adducing the new evidence of our own unbearable pain, and demanding by what right anyone could set them free from retribution. Perhaps it is in acknowledgement of this sense of outrage that Luke places the call

8. *Common Prayer*, 274–75.

## WEEK 2 | UNFORGIVABLE

for divine forgiveness on the lips of one who has endured excruciating personal harm. That suffering gives authority to his prayer for forgiveness from the cross,[9] as it does to his earlier teaching that we should love our enemies, do good to those who hate us, and pray for those who do us harm.[10]

### IMPACT STATEMENT

Like a bomb in a building,
what was done shook the structure,
the whole thing condemned, unfit,
groaning—it collapsed in dust.
Principles? I held some once—
easy enough to proclaim,
until you have to live them.

### AUTHORITY

A kiss that came with a sting
harsh as the lash that cut your
flesh, bitter as mocking wit,
bruising as the cross they thrust
on your shoulder. Your response
to each hammer blow, the same:
these whispered words, "Forgive them."

---

9. Luke 23:34.
10. Matt 5:44; Luke 6:27–29.

## Friday

Forgiving has a terrible cost.

ONE OBJECTION TO THE claim that God's forgiveness is free and offered unconditionally to all, however horrific their deeds, is that such forgiveness is "cheap". This is, of course, a variant of the deep-seated human conviction that anything gained without cost is suspect—if it appears too good to be true, it probably is. All good things, we seem convinced, must be paid for, which is perhaps the mirror image of the fiercely held belief that all bad things must incur a punitive debt. Leaving aside the truth or otherwise of this instinctive human response to wrong-doing and the injuries it causes, we might question the objection to which it gives rise—that forgiveness, freely given, with no requirement to apologize, make restitution, reform, or even request it, is "cheap". Anyone who has genuinely tried to offer such forgiveness and to do so from the heart[11] knows the cost only too well. The price exacted is an emotional pain that can be so intense it feels physical. When we see or hear of people who say they have forgiven those that have done them great harm, we often describe their response as superhuman—somehow beyond the reach of normal humanity.

Perhaps this is a recognition that such forgiveness from the heart cannot be achieved by human means alone. It must be aided by the divine spirit of forgiveness. But for this spirit to encourage and empower us, we need to recognize that God's forgiveness, like ours, does not come without intense pain. God's free, unconditional forgiveness is not cheap—its cost is God's pain. The crucifixion is perhaps an image, a metaphor, a divine acknowledgement of the torture involved in forgiving someone who has done us grievous wrong. How many people have wronged us in our lives? It may be many, but ultimately we could count them. In forgiving the whole of humanity—"sinners" past, present, and to come—God forgives harms beyond any human reckoning, done to God's children by God's children. The torture of the cross reminds us God paid and

11. Matt 18:35.

WEEK 2 | UNFORGIVABLE

continues to pay a terrible price for unconditional forgiveness. God's heart bleeds for us all—forgivers and forgiven.

### RELEASE

I thought I had succeeded,
forgiven, dared to feel proud—
until her cold killer scorned
forgiveness. It made me fume,
the fires once more flaring,
his release—unexpected
meeting on the street again.

### NECESSITY

"Save yourself!" Pilate pleaded;
so said thief and taunting crowd;
even Pharisees had warned,
"Don't go down the road to doom."
Yet he would not let the wings
of death pass by—rejected
only myrrh to dull his pain.

## Saturday

"I'd rather it happened to me."

HUMAN PARENTS, SEEING THEIR children suffer, will often say they wish the suffering could happen to them instead. And sometimes, if circumstances make it possible, they will turn this wish into a reality, for example by starving themselves to feed their children when food is scarce. If a human parent would wish to take upon themselves a pain which had fallen arbitrarily upon their child, how much more would they wish to refrain from being the actual cause of pain to their offspring? Perhaps the crucifixion can be seen as demonstrating that God too would rather suffer than see suffering fall upon us and would certainly not wish to be the cause of our pain through needless punishment. Needless because forgiveness is the simple remedy for our shortcomings, the pain of which falls upon the forgiver, as we saw in yesterday's reflection. The biblical advice not to "spare the rod"[12] has provided an excuse for the abuse of children down the ages. As an expression of loving care for the "correction" of those deemed in need of it, the experience of generations has shown this approach to be an abject failure. Increasingly punitive prison sentences have done nothing to reduce offending, and brutality merely brutalizes both receiver and giver. The suggestion that, "You'll thank me for it in time," is similarly questionable. All that generally results is a growing and hardening resentment towards the one who has meted out the punishment.

The centuries-old view of God as the celestial enforcer is perhaps one reason for the deep and sometimes virulent resentment of the church found among some atheists today. They rail against God, but perhaps it is the picture of God as punitive that has really caused their resentment. The way of genuine loving care is much more effective than retribution in correcting offending behavior, though evidence for this is routinely ignored in a society fixated on

---

12. See Prov 13:24.

reprisal.[13] However, it is God's way. To suggest such an approach as public policy takes great courage; similar courage is required of the church in proclaiming the loving kindness of a heavenly parent who would rather suffer than punish.

## WINTER REFUGEES

Why should you suffer, dear child,
for being born, in a world
of such a bleak, wayward kind?
Take my coat to keep you warm;
take my place in the bread queue
and I'll take yours in the sleet:
take my life—live on my love.

## THE PROOF

All in me is reconciled:
both doer and done-to curled
into my body, entwined
in one twisted, knotted form.
So, I seal the pain from you:
my death, all that can defeat
your doubt, and my loving prove.

---

13. See the work of the Howard League for Penal Reform https://howardleague.org; and Chalke "Punishment".

# Week 3

# In This Together

*Innocent suffering can make us want to punish God. Perhaps God in Jesus accepts this judgement and in sharing human pain holds out a hand to us in solidarity.*

IN OUR FIRST TWO weeks we considered the cross in the context of a punitive and unforgiving world. Now we reflect on it in relation to a world of suffering. Suffering in general and the suffering of innocents in particular are major reasons people reject any possibility that there could be a God at all—especially the Christian idea of God as loving, all-powerful, and worthy of worship. Even those who still retain a vague sense that there is a "greater power" can come to hate this "God" and rail against "him" as manifestly unjust and callous. Such a response to suffering can also be felt by those of a more developed and devout faith. The cross is not an argument or an answer to the problem of suffering, but it may perhaps help to drain away the bile of our anger against God. When we are angry at injustice our human nature seems to crave punishment (see Week 1) so if we perceive God to be unjust, we want to see God punished. In submitting to the cross perhaps God in Jesus is accepting this—accepting the punishment we want to mete out and acknowledging that our response is understandable. In responding to the world's suffering by submitting to personal suffering in Jesus, the crucifixion could be seen as God's way of bowing to ancient Mosaic justice.

## WEEK 3 | IN THIS TOGETHER

If sin is separation, then perhaps one of its manifestations is our separating God from the hard realities of human experience and imagining that God is somehow "above" the things humanity has to suffer, like the Pharisees who place burdens on the shoulders of others but will bear none themselves.[1] In the cross, God in Jesus entered into the worst that life has to offer. God does not claim exemption from our perplexing and tortuous reality and in Jesus suffers a banal fate, not some exalted and noble end: Jesus is just one among countless thousands killed by the Romans; one among countless millions, probably billions murdered by tyrants down the ages. Perhaps it is a mark of the "full humanity" of Jesus that he shares in the full reality of human pain; and when we suffer, personally or as a community, this can offer us a way to reach out for the hand of God in solidarity, rather than pushing it away in anger.

**Monday** On the cross God accepts punishment for what we perceive God has done to us.

**Tuesday** The cross showed Jesus and therefore God to be fully present in life at its worst.

**Wednesday** In being crucified, Jesus shared a banal fate suffered by many.

**Thursday** God suffers with and in all God's creatures.

**Friday** The death of Jesus redeems the human experience of suffering.

**Saturday** If we separate ourselves from God, we are divided from part of ourselves.

---

1. Matt 23:4.

## Monday

On the cross God accepts punishment for what we perceive God has done to us.

WHEN WE ASK A straight question, we expect a straight answer. And when our question concerns injustice we *demand* answers. But is a straightforward answer the only valid response to a question? What if the answer is beyond the comprehension of the questioner or if there *is* no answer? We are hard-wired to seek explanations and not to give up until we find them. And we seem to have a limited capacity for accepting responses to our questioning that are not explanations. There is surely no more burning question, when it comes to considering the nature of God and God's dealings with the world, than the problem of suffering. Writers of Scripture and other theologians down the ages, seeking to speak on God's behalf or in God's defense, have failed to produce a convincing explanation other than that we are being punished. But if God is a God of restorative not retributive justice—a God of endless mercy and forgiveness—then this explanation is suspect too.

Perhaps the cross is not an answer to the problem of suffering but a response that does not offer an explanation. Far from taking on the punishment we consider is due to humanity for what we've done to God, perhaps God in Jesus, by suffering and passing through death on the cross, is accepting punishment for what we consider God has done to us. Perhaps God is offering us the justice of the Old Testament—an eye for an eye, a tooth for a tooth.[2] If the horror of imagining Jesus on the cross doesn't act as aversion therapy (see Week 1, Tuesday) it might cause us to ponder the observation that "An eye for an eye will leave the whole world blind"[3] and also the gospel response to the Old Testament's *lex talionis*.[4] The cross might not answer our questions, but it might help save

---

2. Exod 21:24; Lev 24:20; Deut 19:21.

3. Often attributed to Mahatma Gandhi. It certainly expresses his beliefs, but the attribution is contested.

4. See Matt 5:38–41.

us from the sin of a punitive attitude towards God—and to each other in the face of human suffering.

## QUESTION 1

Why am I here? Why this pain?
And not just now, but again
and again; and not just me
but as far as I can see
everyone in every place
and time. The whole human race
asks, "Who wishes us such ill?"

## QUESTION 2

He, too, is here on skull hill—
flesh shot through with pain like fire,
with each blow screaming higher
till the world is all one scream.
Why? Oh why? What can it mean?
The charge sheet makes nothing clear.
Why is he, too, hanging here?

## Tuesday

The cross showed Jesus and therefore God to be fully present in life at its worst.

WHAT WE MEAN WHEN we say Jesus was "without sin" can be interpreted and explored in a number of ways. Continuing to use the definition of sin as "separation from God", we could say that Jesus is without sin because there is no separation between himself and God. God permeates him entirely—there is no part of his being and experience in which God is not present. Given our own limitations—the sinfulness which separates us from such total union with God—it is hard to imagine what this may be like. But the gospel words of Jesus, "Be perfect"[5] challenge us to aspire at least to bring God into the center and every extremity of our lives. The separation called "sin" could be regarded as not recognizing God's presence in every aspect of our lives. Far from having God at the center of our lives, still less completely permeating them, we relegate God to a corner of our consciousness, to be acknowledged only at special times of our choosing.

If we fail to recognize that being without sin meant that nothing in the being or experience of Jesus was separate from God, then this can lead us to minimize God's presence in the cross experience, relegating it to the fringes. Our sense of God's transcendence and majesty can perhaps make us baulk at the possibility that God could be totally present in the powerlessness, humiliation, and agony of the cross. This reluctance represents a kind of dualism that instinctively seeks to separate the divinity and humanity of the Christ. Apart from anything else, it weakens the power of God's solidarity in our suffering, suggesting that while a human body hung on the cross, divinity was somehow on the margins of the event, perhaps even a spectator. It also, perhaps, weakens our ability to feel that God is fully present with us, when we suffer. We can feel abandoned by God in our moment of need. Even that sense of abandonment is part of the human suffering

5. Matt 5:48.

that the Jesus of the gospels shared when he cried, "My God, my God, why have you forsaken me?"[6] The fact that, ultimately, he was not forsaken is a final affirmation that neither are we in the worst of life's experiences.

### DRAINED

—of light in this pit of pain,
strength ever to rise again,
stamina to carry on,
and last scraps of courage gone—
hope even of an ending
or anyone befriending
such suffering has run dry.

### DEEPER

Even in his anguished cry
a deeper voice was sounding,
like an echo rebounding
from the walls of emptiness
to fill the cave of distress:
one with courage to impart
from an undrainable heart.

---

6. Matt 27:46; Mark 15:34: both quoting Ps 22:1.

# Wednesday

In being crucified, Jesus shared a banal fate suffered by many.

CRUCIFIXION—OR STATE-IMPOSED EXECUTION OF any kind—is not part of contemporary experience in Western Europe. The means of Jesus's death can therefore seem extraordinary—a special fate for a special person. However, the fact that the gospels describe two other victims of crucifixion with Jesus on Calvary that day, "ordinary" criminals, should remind us that a death on the cross was nothing unusual in the Roman world. We might remember the scene in the film *Spartacus*[7] where the crucified bodies of those who had taken part in a slave rebellion lined a road as far as the eye could see. It could be said that the uniqueness of Christ makes his crucifixion unique, but then every victim of crucifixion had their own unique story. Perhaps what is special about Jesus's crucifixion is that, given the status Christianity has accorded him, it is so banal a fate. No special status was claimed in death. Jesus was just one among countless thousands to suffer in this way—he didn't even have Calvary to himself.

Sometimes, in contemporary Western society, those who live privileged lives and to whom material want is unknown can seem to enjoy a special exempt status. Even when some form of suffering does, inevitably, overcome them—through accident, illness, relationship breakdown, financial collapse, bad choices, or simple bad luck—the media treatment often gives their "fall" an exceptional celebrity status. The fall of the mighty is, after all, the stuff of classic tragedy. The fallen hero remains a hero—a special case. But suffering is not special. It is not the exception but the regular experience of life for everyone. The beginning of the Buddha's spiritual journey to enlightenment was realizing this.[8] The privileged, although

---

7. 1960, directed by Stanley Kubrick, based on the events of the Third Servile War of 73 BCE, as a result of which six thousand rebel slaves were crucified along Rome's Appian Way.

8. Sangharakshita, *Who is the Buddha?*, 30–34.

they may never experience a dramatic fall, endure the everyday trials of existence—anxieties, challenges, conflicts, setbacks, illness, and ageing—even if they do so away from the public eye. Although each person's suffering is a unique challenge for them, suffering as a human experience is banal. Perhaps the banal fate of Jesus is God's way of recognizing this and atoning for it by being at-one with it and us.

## CLINIC

Nothing special. Prognosis
bleak. One more diagnosis
in the day's consultations.
Routine commiserations.
"Put this gown on. Join the queue."
Mine was not earth-shaking news.
But still, my world lay shattered.

## ROUTINE REPORT

Nothing special—it mattered
to no one but the dreary
draggle of kin and weary
friends—few and soon creeping home.
Crosses all the way to Rome
from here. No notice taken—
if the earth hadn't shaken.

## Thursday

God suffers with and in all God's creatures.

IF WE ACCEPT THE doctrine of God's immanence, then the divine incarnation of God in Jesus is only one aspect of God's embodiment in the whole of creation. If there is nothing in all creation in which God is not present, there is therefore no suffering in all creation which God does not share. This is not a new perspective. Charismatic French philosopher, theologian, poet, musician, composer, and leading figure in Europe's intellectual revival,[9] Peter Abelard (1079-1142) believed—as did some rabbis—that God suffers with creation. He maintained that the crucifixion represents one particular moment in God's eternal grief.[10]

When asked where God was in the carnage of the First World War, it has become a commonplace for Christian apologists to claim that, to quote a WWI song, God was "hanging on the old barbed wire". We might extend this to say that Christ's side is pierced in every stabbing incident and every human betrayal is the kiss of Judas. But if divinity really is bound up in all of creation, then we have to consider that God feels the damages suffered by the inanimate world as well as the travails of those parts of creation equipped to sense physical or emotional pain. This is more than divine empathy: the cliché "I feel your pain" becomes literal—creation's distress actually *is* God's pain. Perhaps, if fully embraced, Peter Abelard's view of the cross as just *one* example of God's ongoing suffering in God's creation would help save humanity from the sin of placing ourselves and our concerns above God's—loving ourselves more than God. Perhaps a concentration on the incarnate God's agonies in creation, and empathy for God's tears might take our focus away from ourselves and our sufferings and enable us to see them as part of a much broader picture.

---

9. See Armstrong, *History of God*, 236.
10. See Armstrong, *The Bible*, 137.

WEEK 3 | IN THIS TOGETHER

## BLOOD

The bomb blast took us both—hurled
our bodies. I came to, curled
round her, raised her in my arms,
carried her away from harm.
I only realized, once
she was in the ambulance
that my blood was mixed with hers.

## NETWORK

In ancient stones, feeling stirs.
Rent rock, ruptured aorta-
-spurt of magma, fouled water,
choked air, a rogue comet's swerve,
jolt a cosmic net of nerves
whose nexus has always stood
on a hill where nails bite wood.

## Friday

The death of Jesus redeems the human experience of suffering.

THE FACT THAT HUMAN beings can display the ability to suffer nobly does not mean that suffering is in itself noble or to be sought in any way. After all, the Lord's Prayer teaches the followers of Jesus to pray that they might not be brought to the time of trial[11] and the request in Matthew to be rescued from the evil one has been transformed by the church into the more general plea for deliverance from evil. In the gospel accounts of Gethsemane, Jesus is described as praying that the coming cup of suffering might be taken away.[12] However, even if it were desirable to do so, we do not need to seek out suffering—it comes to us unbidden in many ways throughout life. It is a given and, as we have already considered, that fact creates a great problem for any belief in a loving and all-powerful creator God. Our earlier reflections suggest that if there is no satisfactory "answer" to this problem, nonetheless, there may be helpful responses to it.

One such response is provided by scientist, theologian, and priest, Professor John Polkinghorne. He reinterprets the concept of "redemption", commonly applied to the cross, by suggesting that Jesus's suffering and death, rather than paying a debt, redeemed the experience of suffering by sharing it.[13] The apostle Paul makes a connection between our sharing of Christ's suffering and the assurance that through this bond we will also share in his new life[14]—a hint that the bond of shared suffering can bring something new and positive. We might remember examples such as the camaraderie experienced in war. Despite its horrors, suffering has the potential to bring people closer together and transform them for the better. While we remember that suffering is in no way good

---

11. Matt 6:13; Luke 11:4.
12. Matt 26:39; Mark 14:36; Luke 22:42.
13. Polkinghorne, *Science and Christian Belief*, 138.
14. See Rom 6:5.

nor desirable in itself, we can reflect that it may be redeemed by the love that arises when we face adversity with each other and with Christ.

### PROCEDURE

Needle, nurses and their gear.
I clenched my eyes, flinched in fear,
saw an image from TV—
soldier, double amputee,
struggling to walk again.
Though it couldn't stop my pain,
still, it lit me with his flame.

### YOKEMATES

All our sentences the same—
him supposedly a king,
the two of us no such thing—
hung together on one hill.
He's dead already, but still
I can hear his words—so kind:
pledging that our fates entwined.

## Saturday

If we separate ourselves from God, we are divided from part of ourselves.

JEWISH SCRIPTURE REJECTS MAKING any images that might lead to idolatry, especially if they purport to be images of divinity.[15] However, it also claims there is one acceptable image of God and that is humanity itself.[16] Luke's Jesus was perhaps reflecting this tradition when teaching that the kingdom of God is within us.[17] Such insights suggest that there is "that of God" within every human being—a belief central to a Quaker understanding of our relationship with divinity, ourselves, and others.[18] If, as Rebecca Nye suggests, spirituality is "relational consciousness", manifested in relationship with others, ourselves, creation, and the divine,[19] then our spiritual health relies on the proper maintenance of all these relationships. Love of self, therefore, is as vital as any of the other relational dimensions and part of that good relationship with ourselves is dependent on our good relationship with "that of God" within us.

As we have seen, since God in Jesus shared our human suffering, it can be claimed that the crucifixion offers a means of saving us from the sin of separating ourselves from God by hating God for all the suffering in the world.[20] That in itself is significant for our spiritual wellbeing, as it relates to our relationship with God. But the possibility that something of God is an intrinsic part of us gives this interpretation of the cross an extra significance. If we are truly made in God's image and, indeed, God is the "ground

---

15. For example, Exod 20:4 and 23.

16. Gen 1:27.

17. Luke 17:21. Although some translators prefer "among you" or "in your midst" to "within you".

18. See George Fox's letter of 1656, *Quaker Faith and Practice*, §19.32.

19. See Hay with Nye, *The Spirit of the Child*, 109, 115–18.

20. See Spufford, "Creation," 68–103.

of our being",[21] then to hate God would separate us from some essential part of ourselves. If God's sharing our suffering through Jesus's death on the cross can save us from the separation caused by hating God, then our spiritual wellbeing is maintained in two vital areas—love of God and love of the self that bears God's image.

### DIVISION

Wild, unruly, wayward, mad—
they said her paintings were bad
and so was she. Her heart shrank
beneath the barrage. She thanked
her critics. Closed her paint box.
Sealed it behind doors and locks.
Thenceforth, half her world untrod.

### LAMENT

The words of a psalm, "My God,
why have you forsaken me?"
But how could that ever be?
God and our Master were one
before this life was begun.
Yet even with God present,
pain prompts our ancient lament.

---

21. See Tillich, *Biblical Religion*, 81–85.

# Week 4
# Positive Regard

*Rather than being intended to have an effect on God, the purpose of the cross may be to affect us, encouraging self-worth and compassion for others.*

It is an ancient, pre-Christian religious principle that sacrifices made by humanity can somehow cause the gods to do good things for us—provide a bumper harvest, stave off a plague, relieve a drought, bring victory over our enemies, waive their anger for human wrongdoing. This mind-set, deriving from pagan antiquity, has influenced Christian thought and led us to believe that the purpose of the "human sacrifice" of Jesus on the cross was in some way to have an effect on God. If we accept that God's love is unchanging and unconditional, requiring no more of us than the father required of the Lost Son,[1] then perhaps we might consider that the cross is intended by God to influence humanity's view of itself rather than change God's view of us. The nature of that influence may depend on the psychological needs of individuals, groups, or even the predominant psychology of a particular age. In every age and for every individual, however, there is a need to be free from an overburdening sense of our shortcomings—to know that despite them we are still valued and loved. The prayer for forgiveness from the cross is an assurance of this.

---

1. Luke 15:11–32.

## WEEK 4 | POSITIVE REGARD

Love breeds love and to know we are loved and valued can cause us to give positive regard to the one who gives such positive regard to us. Especially, in the context of the cross, we might have compassion for the suffering Christ rather than feeling God in Jesus has received "just deserts" for the suffering of humanity. At the very least, the horror of the cross may act as aversion therapy. Seeing the terrible results of "punishing God" manifested in human terms may help break us of the desire to harm God further, or indeed wish retributive harm on anyone. Viewed at its most positive, by stirring compassion in the human heart the cross may prove our salvation by leading to compassion for all of suffering humanity.

**Monday** The effect of the crucifixion is on our self-image, not on God's view of us.

**Tuesday** We need saving from the psychological burden of our shortcomings.

**Wednesday** Our interpretations of the cross are shaped by our psychological needs.

**Thursday** Are we satisfied by Christ's sacrifice?

**Friday** It is compassion for Jesus's suffering that saves us, not his sacrifice.

**Saturday** The aversion therapy of the cross may turn us away from being hurtful to others.

## Monday

The effect of the crucifixion is on our self-image, not on God's view of us.

Our increasing awareness in recent times that domestic abuse involves psychological as well as physical violence and harm has led to growing familiarity with the term "gaslighting"[2] to describe an abusive tactic in which a person's sense of reality and their evaluation of the world and themselves are systematically eroded. This is achieved by feeding the victim false information. They may be accused of lying or being delusional in their accounts of reality. And any challenge to the abuser, questioning their version of how things are, can be met with the accusation that the victim is the one doing the victimizing. The tactic of gaslighting is not just found in domestic settings but can also be used by dictators and cult leaders. One of its effects is to destroy the victim's sense of self-worth and this can apply not just to individuals but to whole victim groups.[3]

By introducing gaslighting into a faith discussion, I am not suggesting that God is gaslighting humanity. If we believe God to be loving and to have our best interests at heart, that would be absurd. However, it could be argued that the penal substitution model of salvation has fed humanity misleading information by implying that God cannot or will not forgive unconditionally; that the only fitting response to human failing is punishment; and that humanity deserves to suffer for its imperfections. Those who, like the Jesus of the gospels, have claimed God's love is unconditional, or who have defended a more positive view of humanity have often been met with hostility, accused of delusion and charged with abusing the faithful by leading them astray. The cumulative effect

---

2. Deriving from a 1938 play *Gas Light*, developed into a film of 1940 and its remake in 1944 both entitled *Gaslight*—psychological thrillers in which a woman's sense of reality is eroded by a manipulative abuser.

3. Information from https://www.psychologytoday.com/us/basics/gaslighting

has been an erosion of humanity's sense of self-worth. God has not perpetrated this gaslighting. It derives from individuals, groups and institutions who seek to control the narrative of humanity's relationship with God, paradoxically proclaiming the need for salvation from the separation of sin while promoting it by separating humanity from divine love. Perhaps the prayer from the cross for our forgiveness can work to free us from this gaslight effect and re-establish our confidence in ourselves and our relationship with God.

### EROSION

You told me I was rubbish—
faked arrangements, hid my keys,
said I was losing my grip,
protested your love, weeping.
Erosion by stealthy drip
wore away the shape of me—
sculpted to your slaver's wish

### WORTHY

"Do you love me, Peter?"—all
he asks me, as I recall
my betrayals, my sleeping.
My three times, "Yes!" is enough.
He trusts his most precious ones
to hands where red guilt still runs:
"Then feed my sheep." No rebuff.

## Tuesday

We need saving from the psychological burden of our shortcomings.

WE ARE WELL AWARE of humanity's shortcomings—in our news-saturated world, we see daily evidence of our inhumanity to one another, corporate and individual. And if we have any degree of self-awareness, we know how often "We have left undone those things which we ought to have done: And we have done those things which we ought not to have done." But is there really "no health in us"?[4] Surely, we do not need to further "bewail our manifold sins and wickedness"—already, "the burden of them is intolerable".[5] It is often said that the news is over-weighted towards negative stories and does not give sufficient attention to the wealth of good in humanity. The same could be said of the Christian faith. What we need is good news. Matthew's Jesus encourages us to aim for perfection,[6] and the way to get the best out of people is not to tell them continually how bad they are, but to highlight the good in them and nurture it.

What humanity needs saving from is the psychological burden of guilt embedded in the doctrine of The Fall—a doctrine not found in Judaism or Islam.[7] They both view the story of Adam and Eve as Holy Scripture, but neither of our sister Abrahamic faiths read it as producing an ongoing stain on humanity that can only by removed by a blood sacrifice. To be blighted just by being born human is more the stuff of modern nihilism than the doctrine of a faith proclaiming "good news". It is a doctrine that has imposed an intolerable burden and hampered spiritual growth for generations. The unconditional forgiveness proclaimed to the woman caught in

---

4. *Common Prayer*, 35.
5. *Common Prayer*, 271.
6. See Matt 5:48.
7. See Armstrong, *Muhammad*, 99.

adultery,[8] to the Lost Son,[9] and requested in the prayer from the cross could be seen as versions of Unconditional Positive Regard,[10] the beneficial effects of which humanity sorely needs so that we can be encouraged to strive for transformation—repentance—and thereby become the best we can be.

## DAUGHTER OF ENCOURAGEMENT

*for Cecilia*

After many tries, she stands,
wobbly, worry-faced, and then
bump on her nappied behind.
"Oopsy-daisy—never mind!
Up you get, love—try again!"
Soon, she'll walk, to clapping hands,
then, arms wide like wings, she'll run.

## CHARITY

I couldn't keep the thing. Won
it legit—and a seamless
robe's worth having. Nonetheless
I gave it to a pauper.
"You've a good heart—do some good."
As we laid him on the wood
he slipped me that soft order.

---

8. John 8:1–11.

9. Luke 15:11–32.

10. See https://www.simplypsychology.org/unconditional-positive-regard.html

## Wednesday

Our interpretations of the cross are shaped by our psychological needs.

THE SALVATION REPRESENTED BY the cross has been understood in a variety of ways through history and within any given period and culture. As an institution, the church has tended—as institutions do—to seek conformity of understanding. Institutions tend to see divergence as weakening. But perhaps a variety of understandings can give strength instead. Perhaps weakness lies in failing to embrace diversity of interpretation and recognize that through it the diverse needs of humanity may be met. If the cross is a means of liberating us from psychological burdens, the way that it achieves this cannot be uniform because our psychologies are different. If Jesus really did die "for all"[11] on the cross, then all the variety of human need must be addressed by the crucifixion. Wherever we stand around the cross, we must be able to see something in it which will liberate us from whatever is holding us back from enjoying "life to the full".[12]

The interpretation of the cross towards which we lean may therefore be determined by our psychological make-up and needs. If we suffer overly from anxiety, shame (a general sense of unworthiness) or guilt (concerning some specific wrongdoing) then different understandings of the cross may be required to set us free. It has been suggested that "satisfaction" theories of the cross may be favored by those afflicted by guilt; "sacrificial love" may appeal to those who feel shame; and the anxious may prefer "ransom"[13] or "victory" theories.[14] As well as individuals, different historical periods have had different concerns which could be characterized as their predominant psychologies, and these can be seen to have

---

11. Heb 10:10.
12. John 10:10 (New International Version).
13. According to Pruyer, "Anxiety", cited in Watts, "Lenses on Good Friday".
14. According to Watts, "Lenses on Good Friday".

affected their prevailing orthodoxies regarding the cross.[15] If Jesus is Emmanuel—"which means, 'God is with us'"[16]—then God is with us in every age, meeting its needs; and God is with each individual, liberating them from the burdens of their specific psychologies.

### OPTIONS

"Psychotherapy"—Google.
Scan the choice you come across:
Freud, Jung, Reich, Adler, Frankl . . .
Will your mind suit "mindfulness",
"Gestalt", "T-group", "CBT",
find itself in "wilderness",
"psychodrama"—"poetry"?

### INVITATION

Soldiers un-socket the cross.
After-images remain:
dark skies, grave-gape, love and pain,
flogging and a cruel crown,
torn curtain, garden's fresh dawn;
words, like stillness after storm,
"Come and lay your burden down."

---

15. Points regarding individual psychology taken from Watts, "Lenses on Good Friday". For the psychology of different eras see Saxbee, *Liberal Evangelism*, 49–50.

16. See Matt 1:23.

## Thursday

Are we satisfied by Christ's sacrifice?

IN MAY 1373, WHILE seriously ill, Mother Julian of Norwich had sixteen visions of Jesus, several giving vivid details of his passion. They began when she was gazing at a crucifix being held up by a priest who was giving her the last rites. Within days she made a full recovery and later wrote down her experiences in what became her *Revelations of Divine Love*. In one of these accounts she reports that Jesus asked her if she was "well paid" by the way he had suffered for her. She said she was, and he replied that if she was, he was too.[17] It is often claimed that the crucifixion in some way "satisfied" God—this vision of Mother Julian suggests that the key question is rather whether *we* are satisfied by Christ's sacrifice.[18] Sometimes a lover will say to their beloved that they would die for love of them. Julian's vision encourages us to see Jesus's death in this way—not only would he, but he did die for love of us.

Asking if Jesus's suffering "satisfies" us suggests feeding. This imagery is used by the poet-priest George Herbert in his poem *Love (III)*.[19] Herbert describes a host, called simply "Love", asking the speaker of the poem whether they lacked anything, as if the "food" on offer were intended to meet whatever hunger the guest might have. No mention of the crucifixion is made, and Love's concluding invitation to "taste my meat"[20] does not indicate the food's nature, but the Last Supper is inevitably evoked with the broken bread that images the coming sacrifice. Like Herbert, the Jesus of the gospels uses feeding metaphorically when he gives his friends bread saying, "Take and eat; this is my body"[21] adding, in Luke's

---

17. Upjohn, *In Search of Julian*, 82.
18. Argument drawn out in Williams, *Anti-theology of Julian*.
19. Herbert, *Temple*, 316.
20. In earlier centuries "meat" could signify any food, not just flesh, but the association with flesh makes a helpful bridge between the bread of the Last Supper, and the body of Jesus on the cross.
21. Matt 26:26. See also Mark 14:22.

version, "which is given for you."[22] Food builds up, strengthens, provides energy, enables growth, and staves off hunger. Perhaps satisfying all our hungers in the "food" of love is the satisfaction God seeks through the crucifixion.

### FAMINE RELIEF

A small hand against the pane,
cold glass chills the grubby palm,
on the other side, groaning
tables laid to entertain.
Empty belly twists and bites.
The waif jumps back in alarm
as the host looks up, invites.

### SUFFICIENCY

Scraps of bread and wine outpoured
seemed a meagre supper-board
even for us twelve and him.
I heard disgruntled moaning.
But when I saw him break bread
I remembered five loaves—said,
"It will feed to the world's rim."

---

22. Luke 22:19.

## Friday

It is compassion for Jesus's suffering that saves us, not his sacrifice.

IN ADDITION TO THE aspect of Peter Abelard's interpretation of the cross highlighted in Week 3 (Thursday), Karen Armstrong outlines his supplementary insight that contemplating the ravaged body of Jesus moves us to pity, and our compassion rather than Jesus's death is our salvation.[23] This supplies a mirror image of interpretations that see the passion as in some way demonstrating Jesus's compassion for humanity. Rather, his suffering serves as a powerful stimulus to evoke *our* compassion. It is offered as an act of faith on the part of Jesus—faith that his followers will love him sufficiently to be moved by his agony. And moved to the depth of their being so that com-passion— "suffering with"—would be prompted in them.

If nothing moves us to care for others in general, then overwhelming love for one individual may break down our barriers and teach us how to love at least one other person as we love ourselves. A lover, spouse, friend, parent, sibling or child may have this effect on us. The Jesus of the gospels presents those who would be his followers with a stark challenge—to love him more than any other human tie.[24] Perhaps one test of a follower's love for Jesus would be the extent to which his suffering breaks through to the core of their being to release compassion. Does it evoke the kind of compassion that would be aroused by the suffering of a close family member or friend? For Armstrong, active compassion is the unifying heart of all religions, and she advocates an approach to achieving it through a series of steps away from addiction to the ego.[25] Perhaps compassion for the suffering of Jesus as portrayed in the gospels might inspire individuals to begin the journey that saves them from self-centeredness.

23. Armstrong, *The Bible*, 137. See also Armstrong. *History of God*, 236.
24. Luke 14:26; Matt 10:37.
25. See Armstrong, *Twelves Steps*.

## PRIORITIES

"I look after number one.
No-one comes before me—none!
Even my partner, at best
second fiddle to my lead."
Such was my unspoken creed—
until I held my newborn
child against my frosty breast.

## BLOOD BONDS

We clung together in pain—
his and ours seemed all the same,
and hers now mine. I am sworn
to hold her closely as kin.
"Behold, your mother," he said.
To her, "Your son." Beloved,
thus our redemption begins.

## Saturday

The aversion therapy of the cross may turn us away from being hurtful to others.

ON FRIDAY, WE CONSIDERED the possibility that love for Jesus might awaken compassion for his suffering. Today we look at the way compassion for one person may grow to encompass all humanity and become a transformative way of being. As we explored in Week 1 (Tuesday), the horror of the crucifixion could perhaps work as aversion therapy, making us recoil from wanting to hurt God. The book of Zechariah speaks of having compassion on the one whom the house of David and the people of Jerusalem have pierced[26]—an image of Jesus's fate; and in stating that whatever is done for the least of his fellow humans is done for him[27] the Jesus of the gospels identifies himself with all humanity. So perhaps if the crucifixion can cause us to have compassion for Jesus, then by his identification of himself with humanity as a whole, it can encourage us to extend compassion to our neighbors. This would amount to offering them the ultimate positive regard—to love them as we love ourselves. If that could be achieved throughout humanity, then perhaps it would amount to universal "salvation".

The Jesus of the gospels taught that to love our neighbors as ourselves was half of the Great Commandment on which hang all the law and prophets.[28] The other half is love of God, which God's self-identification with humanity in Jesus suggests is tantamount to the same thing. As we have seen (Friday), Karen Armstrong pictures the journey to compassionate living as a progression, and she suggests that the first step is to learn about compassion—"suffering with" others.[29] The compassion initiated by the horror of the cross could provide a powerful contribution to that first lesson. The last of Armstrong's steps is the love for our enemies that the Jesus of

---

26. Zech 12:10.
27. Matt 25:40.
28. Matt 22:35–40.
29. Armstrong, *Twelves Steps*, 21–57.

the gospels advocated.[30] Perhaps the cross can eventually lead to this universal positive regard.

## OVERSPILL

*for my sons and daughters-in-law*

Once in, there's no exit plan
for love: first your own offspring,
then succeeding broods until
their world and its future spill
uncontainable causes
for concern, and everything
and everyone is your clan.

## "IT WAS WRITTEN IN HEBREW, IN LATIN AND IN GREEK"[31]

There came a moment when tears
blurred my eyes. His face, unclear,
the image of anyone
nailed by life's brutal forces.
Anointing revelation,
when he fleshed as one nation
Jews, Greeks—and even Romans.

---

30. Armstrong, *Twelves Steps*, 163–75, and Matt 5:44; Luke 6:27, 28.

31. John 19:20, referring to the inscription attached to the cross on Pilate's instruction.

# Week 5
# Valued Vulnerability

*The self-sacrifice of the cross suggests that unlike human power, divine power lies in vulnerability, offering a view of value that can redeem both individuals and societies.*

LAST WEEK, WE CONSIDERED how a re-interpretation of the cross might challenge the view of sacrifice as something that could somehow change the mind of a deity and induce such a being to benefit their people rather than do them harm. This was an ancient, pagan view of the relationship between humanity and divinity. This week we consider how the cross can challenge another pre-Christian view of the gods: that they need to be powerful, demonstrating the fact by dominance. In the pagan world, the power of deities was linked to the success and power of the nations that worshipped them. Nations adopted gods whom they could consider and portray as stronger than those of their neighbors; and for a people to be defeated suggested the god they were worshipping was weak. God as mediated by Jesus[1] on the cross puts paid to this pagan view. The cross suggests God is vulnerable, but also—especially in terms of the effects of the cross this book explores—that such vulnerability has a kind of power that redefines and transcends our common understanding of the word. The humanity Jesus shares

---

1. The idea that a material reality, such as Jesus in his humanity, can "mediate" the ineffable "ground of being" that we call "God" is found extensively in Caputo, *What to Believe?*

## WEEK 5 | VALUED VULNERABILITY

with us also suggests the possibility that we too can find power through weakness and vulnerability in so far as we are able, like him, to draw on a divine nature that does the same.

The cross demonstrates that to access this power, real not ritual sacrifice is required, and that the personal cost can be correspondingly great. The kind of heroic self-sacrifice exemplified by the cross can transform our view of human potential and worth, elevating our sense of humanity as a whole; and if we truly appreciate what such sacrifice can accomplish it can foster the desire to emulate it. To appreciate the kind of salvation represented by such an understanding of the cross offers a new perspective on human aspiration and achievement. At a personal level recognizing the value of vulnerability can free us from the burden of over-concern about our own well-being. And for humanity as a whole it can lead to redemptive acts that have the widest salvific implications.

**Monday** The death of Jesus suggests God's power can be found in weakness and vulnerability.

**Tuesday** The weakness of the first Adam contrasts with that of the second.

**Wednesday** Accessing the power of vulnerability requires a real sacrifice not a token or proxy.

**Thursday** The cross challenges conventional hero images and hero-worship.

**Friday** The free self-sacrifice of the cross offers a way to freedom from self-concern.

**Saturday** Heroic self-sacrifice transforms our view of human potential and worth.

## Monday

The death of Jesus suggests God's power can be found in weakness and vulnerability.[2]

IF WE REGARD THE Jesus whose bodily reality and physical life are described in the gospels as mediating the divinity that lies unseen in the depth of being, then the material experience of the cross mediates a divinity that embraces vulnerability. If we consider the God who is the ground of being as the ultimate power, then Jesus on the cross suggests that such power can reside in weakness. Looked at in this way, his death can save us from the sin of believing divine potency is simply an exaggerated version of human might.[3] The image of divinity as a greatly magnified version of human triumphalism is one that pervaded the ancient pagan world. It is also a view encouraged by the Hebrew Scriptures in their frequent characterization of God as "Lord of Hosts"—often seen as a military term[4]—and the association of God with Israel's military victories. However, by describing the death of Jesus in terms of a victory[5] Christian Scripture introduces a new interpretation of what it might mean to be a victorious Lord of Hosts.

If we continue in our understanding of sin as separation from God, then the cross counters the sinfulness of separating our concept of divine power from its reality as demonstrated by the Jesus of the gospels. The death of Jesus shows us how far from God's way is the macho approach to power so prevalent in the secular and even the religious worlds. Weakness, vulnerability, and submission are, for the most part, anathema to both. The development of personal strength is promoted in every field of human activity whether it be physical or mental strength, strength of character or of conviction. But in all spheres strength is considered to be demonstrated by the ability to dominate. Even in the area of faith,

2. See Jensen, *Graced Vulnerability*, 26–27.
3. See Williams, *Meeting God*, 62.
4. For example, Isa 13:4.
5. See Heb 2:14.

many would see strength as being shown by intransigence, unwillingness to bend or even consider the possibility that one may be mistaken, and by religious imperialism. The dire consequences of the religious conflicts engendered by this approach are an indication of how far this is from true spiritual strength.

## BETWEEN A ROCK AND A HARD PLACE

*"No Surrender!"* Their banner
bawled a stony defiance.
As the mob rounded the bend
they saw an infant cower
mid-road, as round the far end
marched the counter alliance—
their slogan, *"No Surrender!"*

## THE GOVERNOR

He *made* me proclaim him "king",
declared *I'd* said it. I wrote
it meekly over his head.
He undermined my power—
claimed his entailed no bloodshed
but his own. He did not gloat
to see me bow—amazing.

## Tuesday

The weakness of the first Adam contrasts with that of the second.

IT HAS BEEN CLAIMED that the Adam of the Genesis stories represents all humanity. The Jesus of the New Testament narratives, too, can be seen as gathering all humanity into himself. Paul expresses these perspectives in writing that "as all die in Adam, so all will be made alive in Christ".[6] He even goes on to call Jesus "the last Adam".[7] In both instances he is contrasting the two representatives of humanity. The cross, too—sometimes referred to as "the tree"[8]—can be contrasted with the tree of the knowledge of good and evil in Eden and identified with the tree of life:[9] one leads to banishment and death, the other opens the way to reconciliation and eternal life. Perhaps Jesus on the cross suggests a number of comparisons between his actions and those of humanity in general, as represented by the Adam of Genesis. One significance of the crucifixion could be that it encourages these comparisons and—specifically in relation to vulnerability—that it invites important distinctions between the weakness of the first and last Adams.

When we recognize the weakness and vulnerability of the crucified Jesus as demonstrating a strength beyond that of common human understandings, it is vital that we do not fall into the trap of valuing weakness *per se*. There are varied interpretations of the Eden story. One is that it explores the moral weakness of preferring one's own perceived advantage (the gaining of God-like knowledge) to trusting and abiding by a divine imperative (God's commandment not to eat the fruit). Clearly, it is also possible to regard the Adam and Eve characters' disobedience as demonstrating a laudable independence and inquisitiveness, a critical approach to authority, and an admirable thirst for knowledge. However, it

6. 1 Cor 15:22.
7. 1 Cor 15:45.
8. Following Acts 13:29.
9. Gen 2:9.

is difficult to see how moral weakness—characterized as putting self-interest before all else—could be held to be a strength. The first Adam when faced with the tree in the Garden sought to avoid vulnerability by seeking to be God-like, thus demonstrating inner weakness: the second Adam faced with the tree of the cross embraced vulnerability in obedience to a divine imperative, so showing inner strength.

### MIS-WANTING

I chose not to hear the voice—
clear call to cause commotion,
accuse the bully. Instead
I heard a whispered, "Best wait,"
calculated in my head
the weeks to my promotion,
convinced myself out of choice.

### FREEDOM OF CHOICE

When the crowd at the cliff roared,
"Cast him down!" he chose retreat.
Chose to outfox his foxers.
Chose the time to face his fate,
taking blows like a boxer
with lowered guard, planted feet.
Ordered me to sheath my sword.

# Wednesday

Accessing the power of vulnerability requires a real sacrifice not a token or proxy.

IN ANCIENT SOCIETIES, SACRIFICIAL rituals required a genuine sacrifice on behalf of the individuals and communities involved. The grain, livestock or artefacts sacrificed would deplete the resources of those making the offerings. Sometimes a human sacrifice was ordained. Over time, however, these real sacrifices could become watered down and ultimately tokenistic. We might call to mind the biblical story of the poor widow giving two small coins to the temple treasury, an offering which represented "all she had to live on", compared with the rich people's offerings which were the equivalent of small change—amounts, the loss of which would be negligible to them.[10] But even when a sacrifice of material goods—artefacts, produce or money—represented a genuine detriment to an individual or group, it always fell short of the "ultimate sacrifice" of freely giving up one's own life. Even human sacrifice was the sacrifice of another's life. Not for nothing does the Fourth Gospel tell us that there is no greater love than to lay down one's life for others.[11]

The tradition of animal sacrifice gave rise to the notion of the "scapegoat",[12] which eventually would generate the shameful practice of scapegoating outsider groups, persecuting them as if they were guilty of causing social ills.[13] Worse than sacrificing something of little value, this amounts to sacrificing human beings who are held to be of no value at all. The claim that Jesus "died for our sins" can lead to an association of his sacrifice with the sacrifice of a scapegoat. However, Jesus was not an animal nor, in that he was fully human, could he be seen as an outsider to humanity. The crucifixion of Jesus indicates that for us to realize

10. Luke 21:1–4.
11. John 15:13.
12. See Lev 16:5–15 and 20–22.
13. See Rohr, "Scapegoating".

the liberating potential of vulnerability it is not a scapegoat that must be sacrificed, but ourselves, and the sacrifice must be made willingly.[14] The death of Jesus was not a *ritual* sacrifice—a lamb on an altar—but the *real* sacrifice of a life lived to the bitter end in obedience to God's way. Nothing less was required in order to release the deep power of vulnerability.

## DHARASANA SALT WORKS, MAY 1930[15]

Endlessly, protestors came,
filed to the forbidden gate
where batons broke their bowed heads.
Unresisting, resolute,
time and time again they bled—
flowing blood did not abate
till the Empire died of shame.

## PROPHECY IN THE TEMPLE

Two birds, his parents offered.
Suchlike can never suffice
for this babe to break our chains.
There can be no substitute—
not even his mother's pain—
for the greatest sacrifice:
his own blood, freely proffered.

---

14. See Scruton, *Our Church*, 181.

15. Site of a mass, non-violent protest during the long struggle for Indian independence.

# Thursday

The cross challenges conventional hero images and hero-worship.

THE HEROES OF THE classical world were often those who conquered in the conventional sense. By feats of arms or cunning they would overcome their enemies or surmount challenges in pursuit of a quest. The model was predominantly that of masculine strength, often rooted in military culture, and has continued through Beowulf to Biggles and James Bond. It is found today in the cartoon superheroes whose film representations are accompanied by loud soundtracks and scenes of extraordinary violence on the *big* screen. They are larger than life in every respect. Such characters were also a significant part of the religious literature which was the heritage of Jesus in figures such as Samson, David, and Judas Maccabeus—even the patriarch Abram (later called Abraham) had his warrior moments.[16] Heroes become the subjects of hero-worship, which has this in common with religious worship—the devotee reveres the qualities of the hero and seeks to emulate them, in fantasy and sometimes in reality.

In promoting the crucified Christ as their "conquering hero" the early Christians were presenting a radical challenge to the classical image of heroics. Great heroes such as Spartan King Leonidas might fall self-sacrificially in battle,[17] but this was still in the context of conventional armed conflict and the struggle for the military supremacy of one's own people. Even admired heroics which are not undertaken in a military context, such as "heroic" struggles against illness or the elements, often concern self-preservation and survival. Heroic self-sacrifice on behalf of friends and neighbors in dire need is also revered. But the hero the early Christians proclaimed did not struggle to preserve himself or

---

16. See Gen 14:13–16.

17. Holding off an immense Persian army for three days at the pass of Thermopylae in 480 BCE. According to Herodotus, the Persian King ordered his decapitated body to be crucified.

even sacrifice himself solely for his own people. They maintained their hero had not given up his life in a struggle for personal survival nor for the benefit of his own tribe alone, but for humanity as a whole—friends and enemies.

### TRANSFER OF POWER

Came a day—a season turned—
when my action-heroes lost
their power—just plastic toys.
A pull they could not withstand
stole my heart: its only ploy,
the challenge of love; its cost
the self-image that I burned.

### REBEL HERO

Spartacus—him, I revere.
Took us on and nearly won—
slaves against almighty Rome!
Beaten, he fell sword in hand—
gladiator to the bone.
Not like this sad mother's son—
I poke his side with my spear.

# Friday

The free self-sacrifice of the cross offers a way to freedom from self-concern.

THE BIBLICAL ACCOUNTS OF the road to the cross show that Jesus did not prioritize his own safety and well-being. Even if he did not realize the danger inherent in his words and actions, the gospels show him being made aware of it by others. His disciples tried to keep him from danger in Judea[18] and even some Pharisees sounded a warning.[19] Nonetheless Jesus pursued his aims regardless of personal safety. What those aims were continues to be the subject of debate. This book offers a small contribution to that ongoing discussion. But one thing is clear, the early followers of the Way[20] regarded his sacrifice as having been freely made for the good of others,[21] whatever the nature of that benefit might be. In the recorded actions of Jesus which led to the cross we see the example of someone who was not motivated by self-preservation. Some may have thought Jesus's willing self-sacrifice was mad[22] but although the cross is a punishment meted out to prisoners, and its very nature—fixing a body to immovable wood—is the ultimate in bondage, Christians hail it as a means of achieving liberation.

One profound liberation the cross represents is freedom from the anxieties created by self-centered concerns. Anxieties over personal safety and well-being can become completely debilitating in their extreme manifestations, leaving some unable to interact with what they perceive as a threatening world. And for most people, anxieties about the risks of life can, to an extent, dictate and restrict the decisions they make—sometimes leading to the moral

---

18. John 11:7–8.

19. Luke 13:31–32.

20. A name used of and adopted by the first Christians. For example, see Acts 9:2 and 24:14.

21. The key image being that of the Good Shepherd's willingness to lay down his life for his sheep: John 10:11.

22. See John 10:20.

weakness we explored on Tuesday. Ultimately, the self-restrictions imposed by today's risk-averse society can prevent us living life "to the full"[23]—a denial of the fullness of life which Christians believe is God's desire for humanity. The story of Jesus walking freely to the cross undeterred by danger, is an encouragement to "Live adventurously"[24] and not be in thrall to anxiety. It represents the ultimate living-out of his teaching that we should not worry about our lives but trust our wellbeing to God.[25]

## RESTRAINT

"What voice whispers in my ear,
'Bolt your door and bar your gate.
Don't engage a stranger's eye.
Safety first. Don't be too kind.
Threats around you multiply.
Hold back. Caution. Best to wait.'?"
"Fettered friend, my name is Fear."

## A PHARISEE'S EVALUATION

The lips are lifeless, blue-grey,
that spoke of a good shepherd
giving his life for his sheep.
We said he had lost his mind;
he made his followers weep
when he proved good as his word:
see—the wolves had him for prey.

---

23. John 10:10 (New International Version).
24. A Quaker injunction: *Quaker Faith and Practice,* §1.02/27.
25. Matt 6:25–34; Luke 12:22–31.

## Saturday

Heroic self-sacrifice transforms our view of human potential and worth.

DESPAIR IS A SIN. Theologically, it is the loss of hope in the possibility of our personal salvation. However, even in an age which is no longer preoccupied with eternal destiny, despair can be life-sapping. There is personal despair—a sense of failure and general worthlessness. But there is also "despair of humanity" as a whole. This is particularly the case in the current time, when the media bombard us with horror stories demonstrating our inhumanity. It is tempting to think that it would be better if we simply wiped ourselves out, as it can seem that we are destined to do—to go unresisting to oblivion. As we are beyond redemption, let us simply sink, and the sooner the better, to end the misery we cause each other and the destruction we wreak on the rest of the planet—it would be no great loss.

However, the story of Jesus's willing self-sacrifice presents a counter-narrative. And the Christian faith, in placing the cross at its heart, has based itself on a new vision of human worth and achievement. It is a story that gives us hope and does not just save humanity from despair as it was traditionally defined by theology, but from the modern despairing view that humanity is worthless. The high priest Caiaphas, in suggesting Jesus should die rather than the whole nation perish, was prophetic in a way he did not intend,[26] and the willing self-sacrifice of Jesus saves humanity from perishing in more ways than we might realize. As well as negative stories, the media show abundant examples of heroic self-sacrifice in the bleakest circumstances and the story of Jesus can educate us to look for them and to believe that in self-sacrifice and renunciation humanity can redeem itself. German industrialist Oskar Schindler took great personal risks in saving as many Jews as possible from the Nazi death camps during the holocaust; he also sacrificed his wealth in running a factory whose only product was

26. John 11:47–51.

saved lives. A verse in Hebrew from the Talmud[27] was engraved inside a ring his Jewish workers gave him: it declared that whoever saves one life, saves the whole world.[28]

## METANOIA

Newsfeeds keep me well informed.
Though humanity seems cursed
doctors work as shells explode—
candles flicker every night;
nurses bear their human load—
our best blooms beside our worst:
dab of color—scene transformed.

## HIGH PRIEST'S PRAISE

Better one should die than all—
he seemed to understand this,
said, "I am he," so chose death,
offered neither fight nor flight—
something good from Nazareth!
I could give both cheeks a kiss—
lamb who came to Pesach's call.

---

27. Writings on Jewish law and tradition.
28. Keneally, *Schindler's Ark,* 371.

## Week 6
# Cosmic Transformation

*The cross can be seen as the location for a cosmic battle between the powers of light and darkness which transcends human understanding, the outcome of which transforms our view of existence.*

THE CRUCIFIXION STORIES OF the sky darkening from the sixth to the ninth hour, the earth shaking, rocks splitting, tombs breaking open and the dead rising from them[1] are indications that we should consider this event as having more far-reaching significance than the simple execution of an innocent victim of religious and political oppression. It is of cosmic importance. The darkness recorded in all the Synoptic Gospels steers us towards a view of the cross as the battlefield on which the powers of light and darkness meet in a cosmic struggle. To raise the narrative to this transcendent level means that we are leaving the realm of simple human understanding and its logic. Whatever truth there may be in this interpretation will be recognized by intuition—in heart and soul rather than in the head.

Vital to the significance of the crucifixion in the Christian story is the conviction that it is not the story's end. The cross of Good Friday is the gateway to the new life of Easter Sunday: the empty tomb and the resurrection appearances that follow. The

---

1. Matt 27:45, 51–53. The writer elaborates on the darkness of the other Synoptics to include added dramatic phenomena.

## WEEK 6 | COSMIC TRANSFORMATION

resurrection is the cosmic transformation of reality that, together with the unconditional forgiveness prayed for from the cross, constitutes the heart of the Christian Good News. It represents a new way of being and of relating to God. The old ways, represented by the religious orthodoxy which brought Jesus to Calvary, were defeated on the cross, as was the fear of death. Though darkness fell across the day as battle was joined, the cosmic light was not extinguished: it streamed from the empty tomb and will continue to shine beyond the life of all suns. That is the end without end of the Christian story.

**Monday** The cross is the locus of a cosmic battle between light and darkness.

**Tuesday** Gazing through the "window" of the cross, our view of the cosmos is transformed.

**Wednesday** An innocent sacrificing themselves for another transforms reality.

**Thursday** Old understandings die on the cross: the resurrection brings a new one to life.

**Friday** The cross and resurrection save us from the sin of fearing death.

**Saturday** The death of God is contradicted by the cross and resurrection.

## Monday

The cross is the locus of a cosmic battle between light and darkness.

IN RELATING DIFFERING INTERPRETATIONS of the crucifixion to the prevailing spirits of different ages, John Saxbee claims that the cross as the scene of a cosmic battle between light and darkness was the Hellenistic view.[2] In this connection, it should be remembered that the Hellenistic culture of the Greco-Roman world was the context in which the gospels were written. If the gospels represent the early theological understandings of the Christian community, then Hellenistic views can be expected to have influenced their portrayals of the crucifixion. Certainly the scene—particularly as painted by Matthew[3]—seems to take the narrative into a cosmic dimension. The three hours of darkness may recall the penultimate plague of Egypt which, with the tearing of the curtain, earthquakes, and the breaking of graves, indicates God at work on a cosmic level, reshaping the natural order.[4] These are events that have resonances with images of the "end times" and the fulfilment of God's purposes. They suggest that at the cross God Almighty, the light-bringer, has finally and decisively joined battle with the powers of darkness.[5]

The phrase "the powers of darkness" has been used by writers throughout the ages to characterize forces which they see as inimical to their vision of the good. In this way, like the interpretations of the cross, human understandings of "dark powers" are shaped by the concerns of an age and of particular cultures, groups and individuals within it. It is also common to characterize the struggles of one's own group to achieve "the good" in terms of a greater, all-embracing, universal struggle. We began our reflections in Week 1 by observing that humanity appears hard-wired

2. Saxbee, *Liberal Evangelism*, 49–50.
3. Matt 27:45, 51–53.
4. See Fenton, *St Matthew*, 442–44.
5. See Allison, "Matthew," 884.

for vengeance. This is not, however, the only view of our nature. Karen Armstrong is motivated by the conviction that we are also hard-wired for compassion, and she is a powerful advocate for this element of our makeup.[6] Perhaps, in our own age and culture, the contest between these hard-wirings[7] could be viewed as the current human embodiment of the cosmic battle between light and darkness symbolized by the cross.

## SHADOW SIDE

Fallen petals on the rug—
I chucked the bunch and shouted.
Bedtime stories end in tears
when my patience strains and snaps.
I long to bring light, but fail
and find I side with the dark:
my heart, a cosmos at war.

## SHAKEN CENTURION

Could an iron spike split more
than flesh, fiber, bone and bark?
Heaven's roof cracked by a nail,
darkness flooding through the gaps?
No earthly battle brought fears
like these. What force is routed
here? What hell-deep grave-pit dug?

---

6. Armstrong, *Twelves Steps*, 1–20.
7. Also reflected in Rom 7:19—relevant in all ages and cultures.

## Tuesday

Gazing through the "window" of the cross, our view of the cosmos is transformed.

SPEAKING OF HIS COMING death, the Fourth Gospel's Jesus likens himself to the bronze serpent lifted up on a pole by Moses.[8] The serpent brought healing from poisonous snake bites to all who simply looked at it.[9] If we attempt an interpretation of what the story might tell us about healing, we could perhaps say that looking at the bronze snake was a reminder to the people of the consequence of their wrongdoing—in this case, complaining against God and Moses for leading them into the wilderness. We might say something similar about looking at the crucified Jesus. His teaching on love and forgiveness, even of enemies, leads vengeance-hungry humanity into a "wilderness" in which the thirst for retributive justice goes unslaked and so we complain about it. But when we "survey the wondrous cross"[10] we are confronted with the poisonous consequences of this rejection.

The Jesus of the Fourth Gospel says he will be lifted up like the serpent, so that those who believe in him may have eternal life.[11] The sin of the Israelites was a lack of belief in what God was doing for them. Perhaps the sin from which the simple sight of the crucified Jesus saves us is lack of belief in the transformative, life-giving power of love. There is, however, a caveat appended to the Old Testament story of the bronze serpent. We are told that the artefact was preserved and subsequently had to be broken up by King Hezekiah because the people were making offerings to it.[12] We should perhaps take a warning from this not to turn the crucifix into an idol. The Wisdom of Solomon speaks of the bronze serpent as a symbol—the reader is reminded that the Israelites,

8. John 3:14.
9. Num 21:4–9.
10. Hymn lyric by Isaac Watts, 1707.
11. John 3: 14–15.
12. 2 Kgs 18:4.

looking up at the bronze snake, were not saved by the thing itself but by God, "the Saviour of all".[13] Perhaps we should bear in mind that the cross is not something to be gazed *at* and worshipped, but rather a window *through* which we can gaze at a cosmos healed and transformed by divine, all-forgiving love.

## A HEALING SIGHT

*for Daisy and Ella*

Our universe is transformed—
I am holding hope and light
despite the darkness of life.
I gaze in wordless wonder.
A sight to heal our harsh world:
sweet vulnerability
incarnate in our newborn.

## AN ANXIOUS PRIEST

Exhibit one—frail flesh torn—
proved our culpability.
Heavy clouds above us swirled—
suspense ahead of thunder.
We awaited judgement's knife—
but were spared! With awesome might
earth split. The dead rose, re-formed.

---

13. Wis 16: 5–7.

## Wednesday

An innocent sacrificing themselves for another transforms reality.

THE VIEW THAT THE crucifixion has transformative, cosmic power finds imaginative expression in C. S. Lewis's treatment of Aslan's death and resurrection in *The Lion, the Witch and the Wardrobe*. Aslan the Lion speaks of a "deeper" magic than the Witch knows, which meant that when an innocent victim was willingly killed in the place of a traitor, the table on which Aslan had been sacrificed would split and death would begin to work in reverse.[14] As this is the product of Lewis's imagination, it speaks in his theological language—that of penal substitution. However, it points to a "magic" even deeper than itself in which, when one person sacrifices themselves for another in whatever circumstances, something with the power to transform reality occurs. We may not understand how this "magic" operates, but we can know instinctively that it does. Gretchen Wolff Pritchard claims children can appreciate the transformative nature of the stories about Jesus's self-sacrifice in this intuitive way.[15] And the Jesus of the gospels bids us to be like children.[16] In yesterday's story of the bronze serpent, just *looking* brought healing—no explanation was required.

Perhaps the transformative effect of self-sacrifice is related to the transformation of our reality brought about by love. When we love with all our heart and are likewise loved in return, the world looks and feels different. This is a cliché, but clichés only persist because they reflect a common experience. When we witness or hear of a self-sacrificial act it feels as if we are witnessing this kind of total love in action and the new light on life experienced by those immersed in such a situation somehow spreads out to flood our lives too. The world looks different to us. A case can be made for the view that there is no meaningful reality beyond

---

14. Lewis, *The Lion,* 148.
15. Pritchard, *Offering the Gospel*, chapter 1.
16. Matt 18:2–4. See also Mark 10:15 and Luke 18:17.

# WEEK 6 | COSMIC TRANSFORMATION

our perception,[17] and so if our perception changes, reality itself is changed. There is a blessing which asks that the risen Jesus renew us in the same way that he renews all creation.[18] If the story of a self-sacrificial death which is not the end changes our perception of everything then, for us, everything is changed—all creation is indeed renewed.

### RESULT

I did not hypothesize,
turned up in my heart instead
evidence that all's come right:
negatives need not apply,
nor the universe bode ill—
possibilities abound.
Your love brought about these ends.

### AFTERMATH

When all was finished—his friends
dispersed, crosses taken down,
tomb sealed—it was a changed hill,
a changed city, a changed sky,
changed stars above us that night.
Breaking news of rising dead,
strangely came as no surprise.

---

17. For example, see Grayling, *Wittgenstein*, 117.
18. *Celebrating Common Prayer*, 38.

## Thursday

Old understandings die on the cross: the resurrection brings a new one to life.

THE CRUCIFIXION IS NOT the story's end. It is the major crisis before the resolution of the drama. The resurrection is the concluding scene, and like any satisfying resolution points to a future transformed by preceding events. As we near the end of these reflections and the light of Easter approaches, it is appropriate that our thoughts include the forthcoming resurrection. The gospel accounts stress this was a physical event: although he could appear, disappear, and at times be unrecognizable, the risen Jesus broke bread, ate, and offered solid flesh to touch.[19] What is being narrated clearly has implications for the material world. The resurrection accounts suggest a new set of possibilities for physical reality, having the potential to renew all creation.[20] Probably from the dawn of consciousness, humanity has feared that death is final; and modern physics tells us the ultimate fate of the whole cosmos is utter cessation. The resurrection narratives dare us to consider death may not be the end of our own story; and if so, perhaps the cosmic "death" predicted by science may not be the end of that story either.

For Jesus to rise he must first die. But the manner of his death clearly has importance. Death can occur in a multitude of ways, so the choice of the cross is significant. It was the consequence of the old understandings maintained by the religious authorities—a view of humanity's relationship with divinity that did not recognize the fulness of God's all-forgiving love. The preaching of such love could not be tolerated, nor could the preacher. The old authorities therefore had Jesus executed, thinking they were putting his way to death. In fact, what they had done was put to death their own understandings and facilitate the resurrection, which opened the door to a new, eternal way of being. The cross is the

19. Luke 24:30 and 39–43; John 20:27 and 21:12–13.
20. See Wednesday's reflection.

crisis point of the drama, contrasting the consequences of the old understandings—suffering and death—with the consequences of the new—life everlasting in the embrace of a loving God.

### NO FUTURE

"Clearly the road to nowhere."
"That way madness lies, for sure."
"No hope—no future in it."
We spoke on the balcony,
watching the chanting masses
flow towards the demagogue.
"They're heading for the cliff edge."

### THE DECEASED

"An angel!" "So you allege."
"I fell like a lifeless log!"
"Do you take us for asses?
Such a thing could never be.
Soldier, take a bribe. Pin it
on his friends: they stole him—or
we're the stiffs in this affair."

# Friday

The cross and resurrection save us from the sin of fearing death.

A CLASSIC TACTIC OF OPPRESSORS—be they part of a state machinery, factions within it, or malevolent groups in a society—is to label those they would oppress. Some denigrating word or phrase is devised and applied relentlessly in every reference to them. This is also a favorite tool in political contests. It is even the case that words which are simply descriptive in origin—such as "socialist", "capitalist" or "woke"—can be turned into insults if they are used as such, said with a sarcastic sneer and repeated in this way sufficiently often to lodge in the public consciousness. However, there is a flip side to this tactic. The maligned group can take a term of vilification routinely applied to them and embrace it defiantly for their own use. A well-known example is the adoption of "queer" as a term of proud self-identification by some that the term was originally intended to abuse.

The cross as a means of execution was intended as a symbol of terror, despair, and shame by the Roman Empire. Perhaps the Jewish religious authorities were pleased that in engineering the death of Jesus by this means they would be enabled to characterize him and his followers as people of the cross—crucified no-hopers. Over the course of time, however, Christianity would come to adopt the cross as its "logo" transforming it from a symbol of horrific failure and shame into its universally recognized symbol of hope. This could only work, of course, thanks to something the authorities did not anticipate—the resurrection. As we noted yesterday, one of the most potent and abiding human fears—perhaps, for many, second only to the fear of pain—is the fear of death. Even the resurrection cannot save us from the fear of pain in this life—though God's forgiving love can save us from fear of it in the next—but the resurrection can save us from the sin of fearing death. A bloody corpse hanging on a cross is how his opponents would have liked people to remember Jesus. Instead, succeeding generations have

## WEEK 6 | COSMIC TRANSFORMATION

treasured the combined images of an empty cross, an empty tomb and a dazzling herald of renewed life.

### WRITER'S CONFESSION

I hear the sad evensong
of parting birds; the church chime
rings each passing hour's knell,
"Don't forget me!" is the theme
crying through the lines I write.
Fear of death is testified
every time I lift my pen.

### MISCALCULATION

If we demand his death, then
he's got to be crucified—
they'll hang him high in plain sight.
That sews things up like a dream—
marks him as a ne'er-do-well,
stains his image for all time.
It's win-win! What could go wrong?

## Saturday

The death of God is contradicted by the cross and resurrection.

THE PHRASE "GOD IS DEAD"[21] played a prominent role in religious discourse during the twentieth century, especially the 1950s and sixties. For many, in the aftermath of the Second World War and the subsequent rejection of many traditional social norms, including religious observance or even nominal affiliation, it seemed that for all practical purposes, God was indeed dead. And human experience in the twentieth- and early twenty-first-centuries has made it hard to conceive a loving God could have any life in an age that has seen events of the deepest darkness—two world wars, the proliferation of nuclear weapons in the wake of Hiroshima and Nagasaki, the holocaust and subsequent genocides, 9/11 and its aftermath, and the recent return of war to Europe and the Middle East. If Bishop John Saxbee is right that each age interprets the cross in relation to its own concerns,[22] perhaps our era is most in need of my final suggested understanding of the cross—as a denial of God's demise.

If it is claimed that Jesus is God incarnate then, taken on its own, the cross *looks* like proof that evil can kill even God—the embodiment of love,[23] the source and sustenance of all goodness in the world. And perhaps that, by implication, "that of God in every one"[24] can be put to death. But the resurrection narratives contradict this. They assure us that God has not perished or even retreated from being the incarnate "God is with us"[25]—God enlivening human flesh continues in the risen Jesus and in the hearts

---

21. Perhaps most often associated with German Philosopher Friedrich Nietzsche.

22. Saxbee, *Liberal Evangelism*, 49–50.

23. 1 John 4:16.

24. George Fox's broadening of incarnation: *Quaker Faith and Practice*, §19.32.

25. Matt 1:23.

of Christians down the ages. Despite the expectations of the New Atheists, it has become clear that the death of God—even in the sense of humanity turning its back on the divine—is not going to happen. Indeed, globally God is flourishing despite everything. God, albeit under various names, is still a refuge and strength[26] for multitudes across the world.[27] The conjunction of the cross and resurrection tells a story of darkness and light in which, as the Fourth Gospel puts it, "The light shines in the darkness and the darkness did not overcome it."[28]

## POSSIBILITY

When the shrapnel is flying
"Help me!" prayers can't count for much
if enemies are lampooned.
Our prayers are more distinguished
if their love's unlimited.
See the light in those we shun
and the dead might stir their limbs.

## THOMAS

"Let us go and die with him,"
I declared, and would have done.
But I didn't die: he did—
the light divine, extinguished?
I saw his raw, mortal wounds.
He showed me, saying, "See, touch"—
ten days beyond his dying.

---

26. Ps 46:1.
27. Supporting research is cited in Kemp, *How Far Down*, 69.
28. John 1:5.

## Week 7
# Vistas from Calvary

Wondering about the cross is the work of a lifetime.

THE RICHEST POEMS PROVIDE us with challenges, insights and spiritual sustenance that can last a lifetime, developing with us and fostering our development. The stories associated with the crucifixion and resurrection can operate in this way if we allow them the liberty to function as poetry and afford ourselves the freedom to interpret and respond to them as such. If we do, then we can dwell on Calvary and Calvary can dwell in us throughout our lives, and we can be enriched and sustained by the vistas from that "green hill, far away"[1] at every stage of our spiritual development and growth.

A "mirador", from which this book takes its title, is the Spanish for a viewing point. In English it is used for an architectural feature with an extensive view. The origin of the word is the Latin for "to look at" but it also resonates with a related Latin word meaning "to wonder at". Wonder evokes both awe, imaginative speculation,[2] and, of course, in the context of the crucifixion, Isaac Watts's line "When I survey the wondrous cross". In the cross, Watts saw neither vengeance satisfied, nor wrath appeased, but simply "Sorrow

---

1. Hymn lyric by Cecil Frances Alexander, 1848.

2. It is also a word frequently used in *Godly Play* to introduce open-ended questions that encourage imaginative responses to Christian stories among children. See Berryman, *Godly Play*, 45–54.

and Love flow mingled down." Whatever we see when we survey the cross will color our vision as we turn to look again at the vista of the world from the mirador of Calvary.

## HANGING MAN

> You are your own poem,
> nailed, hanging man—
> dripping metaphors.
> You hold me on this hill.
> Even when your eyes close
> and your ghost is gone,
> I am not.

# Bibliography

Allison, Dale C. "Matthew." In *The Oxford Bible Commentary*, edited by John Barton and John Muddiman, 844–886. Oxford: Oxford University Press, 2001.
Armstrong, Karen. *The Bible: The Biography*. London: Atlantic, (2007) 2015.
———. *A History of God*. London: Vintage, (1993) 1999.
———. *Muhammad: A Biography of the Prophet*. London: Phoenix, (1991) 2009.
———. *Twelve Steps to a Compassionate Life*. London: Bodley Head, 2011.
Berryman, Jerome W. *Teaching Godly Play: How to Mentor the Spiritual Development of Children*. Denver: Morehouse, 2009.
*The Book of Common Prayer*. Large Type Edition. Oxford: Oxford University Press, 1662.
Caputo, John D. *What to Believe? Twelve Brief Lessons in Radical Theology*. New York: Columbia University Press, 2023.
*Celebrating Common Prayer*. London: Mowbray, (1992) 1997.
Chalke, Steve. "The Problem with Punishment." *Church Times No 8449*, 21 February 2025.
Cherry, Stephen. *Unforgivable? Exploring the Limits of Forgiveness*. London: Bloomsbury Continuum, 2024.
*Common Worship: Services and Prayers for the Church of England*. London: Church House, 2000.
Cupitt, Don. *The Sea of Faith: Christianity in Change*. London: BBC, (1984) 1985.
Fenton, John C. *St Matthew*. London: Penguin, 1963.
Grayling, A. C. *Wittgenstein: A Very Short Introduction*. Oxford: Oxford University Press, 2001.
Hay, David with Rebecca Nye. *The Spirit of the Child*. Revised Edition. London: Jessica Kingsley, 2006.
Hayes, Nicky. *What Are You Thinking? Why We Feel and Act the Way We Do*. London: Michael O'Mara, 2022.
Herbert, George. *The Country Parson, The Temple*. New York: Paulist, 1981.
Holloway, Richard. *On Forgiveness*. Edinburgh: Canongate, 2002.
Jensen, David H. *Graced Vulnerability: A Theology of Childhood*. Cleveland: Pilgrim, 2005.

# BIBLIOGRAPHY

Julian of Norwich. *Revelations of Divine Love*. Translated by Clifton Wolters. London: Penguin, 1966.

Kemp, Hugh P. *How Far Down Does the Elephant Go?* Eugene, Oregon: Resource, 2024.

Keneally, Thomas. *Schindler's Ark*. London: Hodder and Stoughton, 1982.

Lewis, C. S. *The Lion, the Witch and the Wardrobe*. London: Penguin, (1950) 1969.

Miller-McLemore, Bonnie. "Practising What We Preach: The Case of Women in Ministry." *Practical Theology* 2.1 (2009) 45–62.

Polkinghorne, John. *Science and Christian Belief: Theological Reflections of a Bottom-up Thinker*. London: SPCK, 1994.

Pritchard, Gretchen Wolff. *Offering the Gospel to Children*. Cambridge, Massachusetts: Cowley, 1992.

Pruyser, Paul W. "Anxiety, Guilt, and Shame in the Atonement." *Theology Today* 21(1) (1964) 15–33.

*Quaker Faith and Practice*. London: London Yearly Meeting, 1995.

Robinson, Marilynne. *The Givenness of Things*. London: Virago, 2015.

Rohr, Richard. "Scapegoating Then and Now." https://cac.org/daily-meditations/scapegoating-then-and-now/ .

Sangharakshita. *Who is the Buddha?* Glasgow: Windhorse, 1994.

Saxbee, John. *Liberal Evangelism: A Flexible Response to the Decade*. London: SPCK, 1994.

Scruton, Roger. *Our Church: A Personal History of the Church of England*. London: Atlantic, 2012.

Spufford, Margaret. "Creation." In *Spiritual Classics of the Late 20th Century*, 68–103. London: Church House, 2012.

Tillich, Paul. *Biblical Religion and the Search for Ultimate Reality*. Illinois: University of Chicago Press, 1955.

Upjohn, Sheila. *In Search of Julian of Norwich*. London: Darton, Longman and Todd, (1989) 1993.

van Gend, Anne. *Restoring the Story: The Good News of Atonement*. London: SCM, 2024.

Watts, Fraser. "Lenses on Good Friday: Anxiety, Shame and Guilt." *Church Times No 8144*, 18 April 2019.

Williams, Rowan. *The Anti-theology of Julian of Norwich*. 34th Annual Julian Lecture, Norwich Cathedral 10 May 2014.

———. *Meeting God in Mark*. London: SPCK, 2014.

www.ingramcontent.com/pod-product-compliance
Lightning Source LLC
Chambersburg PA
CBHW061454040426
42450CB00007B/1349